ASK
SUZE®

. . . ABOUT LOVE AND MONEY

ALSO BY SUZE ORMAN

You've Earned It, Don't Lose It
Suze Orman's Financial Guidebook
The 9 Steps to Financial Freedom
The Courage to Be Rich
The Road to Wealth
The Laws of Money, The Lessons of Life
The Money Book for the Young, Fabulous & Broke
Women & Money

ASK SUZE®

◆

...ABOUT LOVE AND MONEY

SUZE ORMAN

Riverhead Books
a member of
Penguin Group (USA) Inc.
New York
2007

RIVERHEAD BOOKS
a member of
Penguin Group (USA) Inc.
375 Hudson Street
New York, NY 10014

ISBN 978-1-59448-962-4

Printed in the United States of America
1   3   5   7   9   10   8   6   4   2

Book design by Deborah Kerner and Claire Vaccaro

PEOPLE FIRST, THEN MONEY

Falling in love is simple—or so it often seems in retrospect. Sooner or later, however, disagreements crop up, and love becomes a much more complicated business. Can you guess one of the most common subjects of disagreement between couples, married and unmarried? No surprise here—it's money. Everywhere I go, I hear the same complaint: "We're fighting about money." Arguments about money are the catalyst for more separations and divorces than you can imagine. Why? Because people's attitudes and fears about their money give it power—and the ability to wreak havoc on the most important relationships in their lives.

Yet there's a simple answer. I have said it before and I'll say it again: Place people first, money second. Whether you are falling in love, living with someone, getting married, getting divorced, or starting your life over again following the death of someone you love, the people in your life come first. This doesn't mean that money has no relevance to love, however.

Of all the kinds and degrees of intimacy that exist in the world—physical, emotional, social, professional, or domestic—

financial intimacy is one of the most satisfying, and perhaps the hardest to achieve. If you and your partner or spouse haven't walked carefully through all the money matters that might come up in time, I promise you that money will one day become an obstacle in your relationship. When financial change comes to you—and, for better or worse, it will come— it will have the potential to become a minefield of undisclosed expectations or fears.

The following questions and answers aren't meant to scare you away from making a commitment to the person you love. They are meant to demonstrate just how important—and how sacred—a lifetime commitment is and to explain the role that money plays in making it work.

EMOTIONS AND MONEY

Are people really so different from one another when it comes to money?

Yes, they are. How they are different can be very hard to see when you're in love and love is new, and can be very painful to discover after you've made a commitment. But to get an idea of some potential sore points, consider how you've handled your own money as a single person. Have you sometimes spent money that you needed for other expenses and obligations? Put off saving for the future? Occasionally let your bills pile up? These things may not strike you as significant, but when a second person, a fiancé or a spouse, has a stake in your finances and you have a stake in his or hers, undisciplined habits, thoughtless spending, or even incompatible views on how to manage money can strike at the core of the safety and security you want to feel in a relationship.

How can my girlfriend's and my different attitudes toward money potentially be damaging to our relationship?

Start to pay attention and you'll see. Every day, probably without realizing it, you observe how your girlfriend behaves with and reacts to money. You witness the big things, like how she handles her debts, and the little things, like whether she is generous or cautious when leaving a tip. Believe me, if some of the things you've noticed irk you now, they will irk you more over time. In the early stages of love, people tend to overlook what they don't like about each other's management of money; the subject seems at once both too petty and too important for discussion. So most people don't mention it at all. If you find yourself in this situation, you are giving money the ultimate power: the power of silence.

What are the most common problems couples face concerning money?

Most couples *think* they have problems with money for one or more of the following reasons: one partner spends too much while the other spends too little; one partner doesn't care enough about money while the other cares too much; or one partner has too much money, and therefore too much power, while the other has too little. Sound familiar?

In my experience, however, the problems couples face have little to do with money itself. They have more to do with how partners feel about money. Since most of us have been taught to view money as a kind of report card, signaling how well we're doing relative to others, we tend to measure our self-worth by our earning potential, the size and location of our houses, the clothes we wear, the cars we drive, the schools we send our children to, our bank balances, and so on—and not by our thoughts, feelings, and deeds. We value the financial results of our actions more highly than we value the actions themselves or their effect on other people. This is especially true if we have come to believe, as so many of us have, that money is synonymous with security—that money and money alone will provide for us and keep us safe. When our perceptions and priorities are thus skewed and we put money before people, *that* is when we encounter problems in relationships. Talking about money is an antidote. It lays bare some of these underlying issues, and that's how problems can be prevented or solved.

What kinds of financial issues should my fiancé and I discuss before we get married?

You should talk openly about your respective attitudes toward spending, debt, and saving. Be sure not to simply ask (or think), "Who's going to pay for what?" although that's an important question we'll get to later. You and your fiancé should ask each other—and frankly answer—questions about how well you share, how much you tend to spend and on what, how much you save, how you invest, and what your long-term financial goals are.

Start by discussing how each of you feels about basic issues of financial responsibility. Will you support each other in adversity? Do you both view any obligations you may have to your respective families in the same way? How do you feel about respective responsibilities to ex-spouses or children from a former relationship, if any? On a more mundane level, who will manage the household bill paying and bookkeeping?

Be candid about your past and present. Is one of you in debt—carrying a large credit card balance, perhaps, or a student loan that hasn't been paid off? As a couple, what will you do about that? Does one of you have a bad credit rating, and if so, how will you work together to repair it?

Discuss the future. Do you plan to pool your money or wish to keep part, or all, of it separate? What will happen if one of you gets a job offer that requires the household to move—how will you decide whose job takes precedence? If you plan to have children, what will you do if one of you wants to stay home with them? Do you see eye to eye about the financial decisions involved in child-rearing, such as the costs of private vs. public schools? And even though retirement may seem a long way off, do you agree about the importance of investing for the future? Do you have similar goals and dreams for your later years? Are your investment styles in sync?

If you don't start thinking and talking about these issues now, they are likely to become more complicated and difficult to discuss as time goes on. Though you may not be in full agreement on every issue before your marriage, your relationship will be stronger for your having talked through some of your similarities, differences, and concerns.

You say our investment styles should be in sync. Why?
People have different tolerance levels for risk. Some are very conservative when it comes to investing. They want steady growth and a consistent income over the years. Others are willing to accept potential short-term losses on investments that promise greater returns in the long run. Still others are willing to invest in something that carries significant risk if there's potential for a very large gain. But far too many people haven't discussed how much risk they and their partners are willing to take with their shared wealth.

What if my future partner's attitude toward money is very different from mine? Do you believe that people can change their financial attitudes and habits simply by talking about them?

Yes, I do. For one thing, if you can state clearly and frankly what you find admirable, on the one hand, or problematic and troubling, on the other, about the way your loved one deals with money, then your point of view is known to both of you. Second, once you start talking honestly about money, you will be better able to understand the basis of each other's attitudes and behavior. This will help you both compromise on issues of money management. For example, if you know that a partner who seems to be unreasonably reluctant to spend money is probably simply afraid of losing what he or she has—believing that there isn't enough wealth in the world to go around—you may be more patient in your approach to him or her. If you're aware that a fast-spending partner is attempting to use money to compensate for a lack of self-esteem, you and your partner can work together to resolve this deeper issue. The goal in every case is to gradually build a financial relationship that satisfies both of you. Remember, though, that worthwhile changes often come slowly. Promise each other you will keep your dialogue about money going.

My fiancé always ends up getting angry when we talk about money. How come?

The _way_ people talk about money—their expressions, their tones of voice, their timing—can be as revealing as what is actually said. Remember, for most people, talking about money is an intimate and unfamiliar act. If your fiancé gets angry when talking about money, that in itself is a very important key to his feelings about money and may be, at least partly, a result of the way he was raised.

How does a person's family background affect his or her feelings about money?

How people have been raised has a huge effect on how they

view and manage money. The odds that you and your fiancé come from identical financial family backgrounds are pretty slim. I'm not talking about how much money your family or your partner's family had when you were growing up; I'm talking about how the subject of money was handled. Was money a source of anxiety, embarrassment, or conflict? Was it discussed openly? In urgent whispers? Not at all? Did one parent overspend, while the other watched every penny? Did the family pretend it had more money than it did? Do you or does your partner feel embarrassed about your economic background? Any number of childhood experiences can create fear, shame, or anger about money, any of which can inhibit open discussion and wise management. My advice, once again: Keep talking, calmly and compassionately, until you get all this stuff out in the open. Get to know the person you're going to marry in a financial way, and you will know him or her better than you ever imagined. The same, of course, applies to you.

LIVING TOGETHER

I am about to move in with my boyfriend of five years. Do I need to prepare myself financially for this?
Absolutely. Today, many couples—young couples just starting out, older couples who prefer not to marry, and same-sex couples—are living together, accumulating wealth together, and buying property together, and they require many of the same financial and legal protections that married couples have. In some instances, they require added protection, since—if they eventually split up and divide their assets—they have few of the automatic legal protections that married couples have.

A note: Some unmarried couples choose not to marry

because they dislike the prospect of being bound by a legal contract. Some think marriage is just a formality; others have been married and burned, and don't want to make the same mistake again. Whatever your reasons for not marrying, you should be aware that without a written agreement, you may be legally vulnerable in a number of ways.

How am I vulnerable if I live with someone without an agreement?

To take a typical case, consider what might happen if you and your live-in partner decide to buy a home together. If your partner is making a larger contribution to the down payment than you are, it may seem to make sense to hold the property solely in your partner's name. But if you split up, guess who gets the house? Your partner does. Or say that both names are on the title, although you contributed a larger amount for the down payment. What happens if you split up? You could lose your larger share and only get half. Or perhaps you assume you have the rights of joint tenancy with your partner—meaning that if your partner dies, 100 percent of the house will go to you. But when he dies, you discover that you misread the title and that instead of being a joint tenant, you are a tenant-in-common. This means that your partner's share of the house goes directly to his estate, which he may have left to his younger brother. By law, the brother can move in with you. Property can become a troublesome issue without a contract.

Are there any other problems I can get into without a contract?

Yes, especially if you separate. If you have been financially dependent on your live-in partner, for example, without a contract you will have no legal right to receive ongoing financial support from him or her. Also, you may have no right to share in any of the assets your partner may have accumulated, perhaps with your help, during the years you lived together. This may or may not come as a surprise to you, but it has caused real grief to many longtime partners who assumed they would be provided for, but weren't.

Other issues can arise. What if your partner becomes sick, so sick that he or she can't make medical decisions? He or she may have expressed to you a firm wish not to have any extraordinary medical measures taken. Well, guess what? If your partner's closest blood relative wants to have him or her hooked up to a ventilator, you have no legal right to stop it. And what if you and your partner have agreed that you will inherit each other's estates in the event either of you dies? Without a will, in the eyes of the court, you are not your partner's legal heir, as you would have been if you were married.

Is there any way I can protect myself financially while my partner and I are living together?

Yes. But before we get into cohabitation agreements, there are a few basic things that you should do. First, make all your financial expectations and intentions very clear to your partner. If you give him or her $500 as a birthday gift, write the word "gift" on the check so that, in the worst-case scenario, a court will not view this check as evidence of a promise to support your partner. If you make a loan that you expect to be repaid, write "loan" on the check. Never put money in a joint account just because you think it will add trust or convenience to your relationship, and don't put both names on a title unless you truly want to be *joint* owners, by which I mean fifty-fifty.

Why do you advise against putting my partner's name on my accounts?

If your partner ever filed a palimony lawsuit against you, a joint account or joint ownership of property could be viewed by the court as powerful evidence of an understanding between the two of you to share everything. In some states, including California, the courts make decisions on the validity of cohabitation agreements if there seems to be an "implied" agreement between the two partners. (I'll say more about this later.) In other states, a written agreement is required.

My boyfriend and I are about to move in together and probably will get married. Should we merge our expense money or keep it in separate accounts?

You may want to merge the money you earmark for common expenses that you fund on a monthly basis. Otherwise, I'd advise you to keep separate accounts for your individual personal expenses, savings, and investments. I recommend this for legal reasons, but I also suggest that married couples keep personal discretionary money in individual accounts. The reason: You two are individuals with separate identities. Your money is an integral part of who you are. When you marry or live together, you're creating a new, third entity—a partnership—that deserves a bank account of its own. Apart from the financial obligations you assume together, you each have a right to decide how and when to spend the money you've earned.

Should we have joint credit cards?

No. Keep separate credit cards, so as to establish your own credit record, now and for the future.

What sort of account do you suggest my fiancé and I open jointly?

Many mutual fund companies allow investments of less than $1,000. And if you set up a monthly Automatic Investment Plan, you can invest as little as $25 or $50 a month.

How should we determine who contributes what to cover our monthly expenses?

I always recommend making your respective contributions in proportion to your current wages, salary, and other income. Here's how to do this: Let's say that your joint expenses, including rent, utilities, food and other household goods, entertainment, and maintenance will come to about $3,500 a month. (When estimating your monthly costs, always add an extra 10 percent for unexpected expenses, now and down the line.) Add together the monthly income that you and your partner each bring home, after taxes and retirement savings. Let's say that figure is $7,000. Now divide the total of your joint expenses, $3,500, by the total of your joint take-home pay ($7,000). This gives you the percentage (50 percent) of your take-home pay that each of you should contribute to your joint account—that might be $3,000 a month for you, and $500 for your partner. Of that $3,500, you'll use $3,181 to pay your bills and $318 for emergencies.

COHABITATION AGREEMENTS

How can I avoid legal and financial complications if I am planning to live with someone?

There is a very good answer to that question. I suggest that you and your partner ask your lawyers to draw up a cohabitation agreement. This is simply a written document that states your mutual rights and obligations with respect to joint and separate property, as well as any other financial obligations or expectations you wish to agree on in advance of moving in together. If you discover that you and your partner have different ideas about the financial aspects of living together, it's better that you find out now rather than later.

Can't we just draft this agreement on my computer? Does it have to be prepared by an attorney?

You can draft a cohabitation agreement yourselves, but each partner needs to have their own, separate attorney review it. Attorneys can identify any loopholes or mistakes of law. Plus, if one partner alone creates the agreement and it's not reviewed by legal counsel, the terms of the agreement could later be thrown out by a judge in court.

Why should we each have our own attorney?

For the same reason people should have separate attorneys when drawing up a prenuptial agreement (more about these later). If your cohabitation agreement comes before a court, the court might question its validity if it appears that either one of you has not been fairly represented by counsel. This is especially true if a lot of money is at stake.

Do courts really honor cohabitation agreements?

Almost every state in the union honors *written* cohabitation agreements. Many states will consider oral or implied agreements, but since memories often differ during the dissolution of a relationship, it can be very hard to prove a point made by an oral agreement.

What is an implied agreement?

The court defines an implied agreement as a pattern of actions or conduct suggesting an unspoken understanding between the two parties in question. Such actions or conduct may include owning joint property, maintaining a shared checking or savings account, or a history of one partner working and the other staying at home. If you have been financially supporting the woman you live with for some time and the two of you break up, a court could find that the two of you had an "understanding" that this state of affairs would continue—even if no such understanding was put into words.

How about an oral vs. a written agreement?

An oral agreement is exactly that—an actual exchange of spoken words with a clear agreement reached. It's better to have it on paper—that's my advice. Written agreements are superior to oral and implied agreements. They are more specific about date and content, and they provide more peace of mind. In the worst case, they will clarify for a court the nature of your intentions when you drew up the agreement. Even better, they offer you and the person you love a chance to go over your finances with a fine-tooth comb, eliminating possible future areas of disagreement or misunderstanding.

SAME-SEX COHABITATION

What's the legal difference between same-sex cohabitation and heterosexual cohabitation?

Legally, there's no difference. As unmarried partners, you, like unmarried heterosexual couples, lack the legal protections that marriage automatically confers, so you have to create these legal safeguards for yourselves.

Remember, you cannot rely on a family court to protect you or assist in dividing up your property if you separate; there is no jurisdiction in this country that will automatically recognize your inheritance rights. Further, if you have children, you cannot collect child support and you cannot appeal to the judicial system for custody or visitation (except in those few places where a same-sex partner can adopt his or her partner's children). Even more than heterosexual couples—who can, after all, get married in a pinch—gay couples in serious relationships should have some or all of the following: wills, living trusts, health-care proxies, durable powers of attorney, and written agreements about the disposal of jointly owned property. Though some of these agreements may not be fully enforceable in many jurisdictions, they do provide a framework to guide your actions at times when you may be emotionally overwrought and unable to make sound, fair decisions.

In 2004, Massachusetts became the first state to grant same-sex couples the right to marry, which entitles the couple to all the rights under state law. Marriage is the only category that offers full recognition of spousal rights for same-sex couples and heterosexual couples equally. California, Connecticut, New Jersey, and Vermont have established either domestic partnerships or civil unions, which make the couple subject to all the same family-law rules that apply to married couples under state law. Other states may adopt similar laws in the future.

It's especially important for you to put everything in writing. In just about every state, written *and* oral contracts between unmarried couples—including same-sex couples—are, hypothetically anyway, legally binding. But oral contracts are hard to prove, and in some parts of the country, a gay or lesbian partner may find it exceedingly difficult to enforce the terms of an oral or an implied agreement in court.

How should we draft a cohabitation agreement?

There are several excellent books to help you get started, including *Living Together: A Legal Guide for Unmarried Couples* by attorneys Ralph Warner, Toni Ihara, and Frederick

Hertz; and *A Legal Guide for Lesbian and Gay Couples* by attorneys Hayden Curry, Denis Clifford, and Frederick Hertz. Further, if you have significant assets, you should consult a qualified attorney. I know a gay couple who went so far as to make a videotape of themselves stating their intentions in front of a lawyer, to be sure that no one in either of their families could challenge the rights they had granted to each other.

I am in a same-sex relationship, and my partner and I own property together. What happens in the event we break up?

If the property is held jointly, either party can petition the court to sell the property and divide the proceeds of the sale according to the terms of an agreement, or fifty-fifty in the absence of an agreement. The partners can also try to reach an amicable agreement between themselves by putting the property on the market and dividing the proceeds of the sale, or one partner can buy out the other's share.

My partner's name is on the title of the house we are living in together, but I have been paying the mortgage. Now we are breaking up. Do I have any rights to the property?

The property will go to the partner who holds title, unless the unnamed party can claim that he or she had an agreement with the partner to share the asset. (In some states, only written agreements can supersede the title.) The dispute will be resolved in the ordinary "business" division of the local court, rather than the family law division, and contract law rather than family law will apply.

If my partner and I haven't bought property together, are we financially obligated toward each other in any way?

It depends on whether you've signed an agreement specifying obligations to each other. If you wish to formalize a set of financial obligations, it's better to have a written contract.

Can my same-sex partner and I enter into a common-law marriage?
No. As of this writing, common-law marriages don't extend to same-sex couples. And so far, only Massachusetts offers formal recognition of same-sex marriages. Vermont, New Jersey, and Connecticut offer same-sex couples the option to enter into civil unions, and California allows same-sex couples to register as domestic partners, which gives partners many rights. Hawaii, Maine, and the District of Columbia also provide some domestic partner benefits.

COMMON-LAW MARRIAGES

What exactly is a common-law marriage?
Some states—currently there are 14, plus the District of Columbia and, to a limited extent, New Hampshire—legally recognize that a man and a woman who have lived together for a sustained period of time, and who think of themselves and present themselves to the public as man and wife, are joined in "common-law" marriage within that state and are entitled to the protections of marriage. Since the marriage is not formally recorded, however, the burden of proof is with the couple—or one partner.

What kind of proof do you need to show that you are in a common-law marriage?
The laws differ from state to state. In general, partners must prove that they have the mental capacity to marry, and they

must have lived together under one roof for a significant period of time (this period is not defined in any state). They must share the same last name, refer to each other as "my wife" and "my husband," and file joint tax returns. Their friends and acquaintances also must consider them to be "married."

If you are in a common-law marriage and it breaks up, do you file for divorce the same way you would if you were formally married?
Yes.

Do marital rights automatically accrue to a person who lives with you as a spouse over a long period of time, even if you are not formally married?
Only if you live in one of the states that honors common-law marriages. In many other states, you can consider yourself to be husband and wife, file joint tax returns, and so on, but if you're not legally married you have no rights if your partner dies or leaves. It's even possible that if your partner were in an intensive care unit, you wouldn't be allowed to visit in a non-common-law state—because you would not be considered "next of kin." Establishing a durable power of attorney for health care ("durable" because it remains in effect even if you become incapacitated) is the only way to protect yourself against this possibility.

I am 58 years old and I have lived in a common-law marriage with my partner for many years. Does Social Security make any allowances for us?
In general, no, though there are a couple of ways in which you and your partner could achieve dependent status under Social Security Administration rules. The first is if one of you adopts the (age 18 or younger) child of the other one. The second is

if you and your partner live in a state that honors common-law marriages.

Which states currently recognize common-law marriages?

In no particular order, the states are Oklahoma, Pennsylvania, Rhode Island, Alabama, Colorado, Iowa, Kansas, South Carolina, Texas, Utah, Ohio, Georgia, Idaho, and Montana, as well as the District of Columbia, and for inheritance purposes only, New Hampshire.

PRENUPTIAL AGREEMENTS

What exactly is a prenuptial agreement?

A prenuptial—or premarital or antemarital—agreement is a legal contract entered into before marriage that specifies how a couple's assets and debts are to be divided in case of a divorce. A pre-nup can also delineate certain expectations partners bring to the marriage, i.e., which partner will work, which partner will stay at home with the children, and various inheritance rights. Think of it as the best way to ensure your financial security in the future.

I thought pre-nups were just for rich people.

You are not alone. Years ago, pre-nups were primarily used by people who had considerable wealth that they wanted to protect. Even now, the pre-nups we tend to hear or read about are those signed by movie stars or others with many assets. Yet these days, pre-nups are very common among people of ordinary means. Most women and men have assets they wish to protect—or the prospect of future assets they want to make secure plans for. In fact, people with very few current assets may enter into a pre-nup in order to protect future earnings or inheritances, or to shield against future debts incurred by a spouse who may prove to be financially irresponsible. Ultimately, a well-written pre-nup can protect you no matter what financial circumstances arise.

I'm still not convinced I need a pre-nup. Can you give me some examples of situations in which someone would want to have one?

Yes. Here are some scenarios in which pre-nups would be useful. You and your spouse-to-be both work, and you decide you want to keep future earnings or stock options separate. You put that in the pre-nup. One of you has previously been through a bitter divorce, and you know how painful, divisive, and expensive wrangling over marital property can be, so you determine any divisions beforehand and record them in a pre-nup. You've inherited an extensive portfolio from your parents, a portfolio that may take you—and possibly your spouse—a lot of time and effort to manage. You will both reap the rewards during your marriage. Even so, you want to make sure that this portfolio and its growth remain in your name alone should the marriage dissolve. That, too, goes in a pre-nup.

I know that one day I'm going to inherit my parents' vacation home. Since my folks no longer use it very much, my fiancé and I have begun spending weekends there and are full of plans to fix it up together. Still, this house has been in my family for several generations, and I want to make sure it remains in my family. Is this something a pre-nup can cover?

It certainly is, and it's a perfect example of the protection a pre-nup can provide. A pre-nup is a good idea whenever you want to ensure that an asset—whether property, an equity stake in property, securities, valuables, or a retirement plan—is protected.

Isn't it kind of insulting to tell the guy I'm going to marry that I want a pre-nup? Won't he think that I don't have much confidence in our future together?

That's a common worry, but if the safety, happiness, and general welfare of both partners is a clear priority for each partner, negotiating a pre-nup will be seen as a mark of respect for yourself, your partner, and the financial future you will have together. Moreover, it's an opportunity to express your most intimate concerns about money, security, child-rearing, and other issues—and to do so before marriage's normal challenges and problems cause emotions to run high. In my experience, talking honestly about money and the future brings partners closer together. If this is important to you, my advice is to let your beloved know how you feel. Chances are that he will want you to be protected and to feel safe, just as you want him to be.

OK, you've convinced me. How do I go about getting a prenuptial agreement drawn up?

One thing *not* to do is rely on one of the many "how-to" CD-ROMs for creating your own prenuptial agreement. Computer programs and resource books are a good starting point for a discussion with your partner, but after you've both jotted down some notes, ask a good attorney to draft your agreement according to the laws of your state. Pre-nups made with a CD-ROM are too easily contested—do-it-yourselfers beware!

Before signing a pre-nup, each of you should consult a separate attorney to make sure that the final agreement works for each of you. This may seem awkward, but it allows you to express any remaining concerns privately, acts as a final protection against oversights, and can prevent confusion later on.

Are we required by law to have separate lawyers?

Yes, in some states separate legal representation is required for the agreement to be valid. Even where separate representation isn't required, it can smooth a separation settlement by weakening any claim by either of you that you did not know what you were signing, did not understand the agreement, or were unfairly represented by counsel. Your lawyers should sign the agreement as well, to show that they have reviewed it carefully.

How should I prepare for this meeting? What will the lawyers who are drawing up my pre-nup want to know?

Several things. First, it is very important that you and your partner disclose to each other all of your assets and liabilities. Full disclosure is essential and will include all respective property, income, debts, obligations and expenses, and anything else that will affect the value of your estate, now or in the future. Second, you and your partner must agree that you are entering into the pre-nup freely and without undue coercion. Courts can be very sensitive to the issue of coercion. If one partner is deemed to have exerted undue pressure on the other to sign, a pre-nup can be overturned. Also, the terms of the pre-nup must be fair.

What does "fair" mean in this context?

In this context, "fair" means that the agreement takes into account your age, your partner's age, your state of health, your job, your income, your standard of living, your family responsibilities if applicable, and your preexisting assets, whether these include real property, an investment portfolio, an insurance policy, or anything else of value. You and your partner must show evidence that you understand all of each other's assets and income. Sometimes, your lawyers will suggest that you or your partner bring copies of recent tax returns, monthly statements from a brokerage firm, or other financial documents that could affect the pre-nup. Also, you must both show that you fully understand the legal and financial consequences of the agreement. If a court later deems the agreement unfair or incomplete, it can be thrown out.

What, exactly, is the definition of property?

In most courts of law, property includes everything from your old coin collection to your retirement funds. It also includes your car, your boat, your furniture, your jewelry, your house, any debts, patents, book or music royalties, intellectual property (such as novels and screenplays), artwork—you name it. Property basically includes everything you can think of, other than human beings.

What else does a pre-nup include?

It can include almost anything that does not violate public policy. Future debt, future stock options, future retirement benefits—all can be designated. There have been pre-nups that cover who will get the baseball season tickets and who will feed the dog.

Is there anything that can't be put in a pre-nup?

Issues that touch on child custody and child support in a pre-nup will not be binding in court. Anything that appears to anticipate illegal actions (such as illegal gambling or even murder) are not enforceable, and the same goes for anything that binds one or the other partner to obligatory sexual duties. (Courts don't want to enforce sexual duties, for obvious reasons.) Any agreement that would leave a spouse totally destitute or a ward of the state is also unenforceable.

Can a pre-nup replace our wills and living trusts?

No. The chief intent of a pre-nup is to cover what happens in the event of a dissolution, not a death.

Do all 50 states recognize pre-nups?

Yes. There is a nationwide Uniform Prenuptial Agreement Act (UPAA). The particular laws of each state may differ as to the conditions for enforcing a pre-nup, but even community-property states—which mandate dividing marital assets and debts fifty-fifty at divorce—recognize the primacy of a pre-nup that specifies the division of property or debt in another way.

Do judges pay attention to pre-nups? If they don't, is it worth asking my fiancé to sign one?

Until recently, judges were not all that favorably inclined to enforce pre-nups. Years ago, many states did practically everything they could to discourage divorce. Courts in those states tended not to honor pre-nups, because pre-nups, they believed, planted the idea of divorce in partners' minds. Well, times have changed. Most judges now have come to recognize that some couples may be better off divorced—and if they do divorce, they are much better off for having signed a pre-nup. Generally speaking, courts now enforce these agreements. Exceptions include contracts the court views as giving one spouse a powerful incentive to end the marriage, for example, if a spouse is entitled to more money if the marriage lasts a certain number of years (they see this as promoting divorce, which they still look unfavorably upon). Agreements that are viewed as a contract to evade creditors illegally, or, again, that the court believes one party intimidated the other into signing, are viewed unfavorably.

Where and when will we sign our agreement?

You'll probably sign your pre-nup in a lawyer's office and, in the best case, you'll sign at least six to twelve months before your wedding date. I will tell you this much: Don't sign on the way to the wedding! Courts will invalidate a pre-nup if they find that both parties did not have ample time to think about what they were signing.

Do pre-nups have to be witnessed and/or notarized in order to be valid?

Rules vary from state to state. In New York a pre-nup must be notarized to be valid. In other states neither witnesses nor notaries are necessary. Your attorney(s) will be aware of the requirements in your state.

How much does it cost to draft a pre-nup?

The cost varies from a couple hundred dollars to several thousand dollars for financially complicated agreements—still not much when you consider that a bitter divorce can cost tens of thousands of dollars and take years to resolve.

What if we want to make some changes after the contract is drawn up and signed?

This isn't a problem. You will follow the same procedure you used when you had the contract drawn up in the first place. Have the agreement witnessed and notarized, if necessary, and state expressly whether you're replacing the earlier document with this one or simply amending certain terms listed in the previous agreement. If you draft an agreement *after* you are married, it is technically known as a postnuptial agreement.

The enforceability of postnuptial agreements varies from state to state.

If we draw up a pre-nup in one state and then move to another state, is the pre-nup still valid?

Not always, and possibly not in every detail. Have your original contract reviewed by a good attorney in the new state. If anything needs to be changed, he or she can make those changes. Be aware, however, that enforceability of postnuptial changes, like postnuptial agreements, varies from state to state.

If we have a pre-nup that divides our property differently from what is dictated by the laws of our state, will our pre-nup stand?

In most cases, yes. If the contract is drawn up correctly, your agreement will allow you to modify or even wriggle out of the state property system, even if you live in a community-property state. Then you can implement an agreement that better suits your needs.

We've been married for more than 20 years and so much about our financial situation has changed since we first drew up our prenuptial agreement. Should we change the pre-nup or should we just dissolve it? It seems like there's no reason to have one anymore.

I don't think you should ever dissolve your pre-nup. Changes in your financial status, which may strike you as a reason to abandon your pre-nup, can easily be accounted for in an amended agreement. (In the best case, such changes will have been anticipated in the original document, *if* it was drawn up correctly.) The primary reason you have a pre-nup is so that you and your spouse will have assurance that both of you will be protected, whatever may come. "Whatever may come" is a key phrase here—you never know what the future holds, so why risk exposing yourselves to the unknown by dissolving a protective agreement? Have it amended instead.

I'm a widow with three children from a previous marriage, and I am getting married again next spring. Should I get a pre-nup?

Certainly, if only to protect your children. Without a pre-nup, your new husband will acquire a legal right to inherit at least a portion of the assets you may intend for your children to inherit. A pre-nup is especially important for widows (or widowers) who want to protect a deceased spouse's money for the children. It's also a useful instrument to soothe grown children's suspicions or ease resentments about a new stepparent; it demonstrates that any assets due to go to them will be protected for their use.

PRE-NUPS AND DEBT PROTECTION

Without a pre-nup, am I responsible for debts my spouse incurred before we were married?

In most cases, you are not responsible for such debts. You may, however, be responsible for debts incurred during marriage. If you and your spouse have a joint credit card issued in both your names, for example, you are each responsible for all debt on that card.

What happens to me if the credit card my spouse uses is issued only in my spouse's name?

That's trickier. Let's consider credit cards that your spouse has in his or her name alone, for his or her own purposes. If your spouse creates a large debt and cannot pay, the creditor has a legal right to come after you—unless you have filed a pre-nup with the credit card company stating that you are not responsible for your spouse's separate debts. Why? Because your partner probably checked "married" in the marital status box on the application, and thus triggered a clause, in very fine print, stating that the cardholder's spouse will also be responsible for the debt, unless otherwise noted.

Can a pre-nup give me protection against most of my partner's debts?

In some states, you can protect yourself by having a pre-nup that specifies which debts you will not be responsible for. For example, you could state that any credit cards in your spouse's name alone will not be your responsibility. This option may or may not be available in your state. Check with a lawyer to see whether sending a copy of your prenuptial agreement to all pertinent credit card companies, including those with which you set up new accounts, will afford protection.

MARRIAGE AND MONEY

My husband and I have been married only six months, and already we're squabbling about finances. He spends money on computer equipment. I spend money on household goods. He insists on paying the bills and then forgets to do it. I feel as if a gap has opened up between us. You're in good company. Building a shared financial life is a challenge. Most single adults have clear, even entrenched, financial housekeeping preferences—some balance the bank statement every month, others balance it once a year or not at all. Some pay the bills as soon as they come in, others don't mind being late. The challenge is in devising a plan that will work for both you and your partner.

First things first. No matter who pays the bills, it's important that you both be familiar with everything about your finances. You should know the monthly costs of food, clothing, shelter, insurance, car loans, and more. If you have children together, you should have calculated how much their education is going to cost. You should each be aware of how much the other partner is spending each month on items in your joint budget, how much each of you is saving for retirement, and what securities the other holds in investment accounts. This is the only way for you to be respectful of the money you have in common—and respectful and protective of each other in your essential role as partners.

To answer your question, why not consider paying the bills together every month? If that doesn't work for you or makes you crazy, one of you might do it one month and the other the next, or switch every six months. Ideally, you should both think about, touch, and manage your money.

What about spending money? That's where my wife and I have the biggest arguments.

Spending and bookkeeping go hand in hand. The best strategy is to sit down together and draft a spending plan or budget. Together, decide how much of your joint income you will devote to discretionary spending after necessities have been paid for. Make policy decisions. How often will you get a new car? How many vacations will you take this year, and what will they cost? How much will you spend during the holiday season? What percentage of your income will you save for retirement or give to charity? Agree on or compromise over what you need, want, and can afford. Develop a shared vision for the future, and a means of getting there. Remember, both of you, working with small sums of money over time, can create a great deal more wealth and security than either of you could alone. The key is to work together.

Is there any advantage to trying to keep our money separate by filing separate tax returns?

In most cases, no. One exception involves child and spousal support from a previous marriage. In some states, including California, an ex-spouse's tax return can be subpoenaed by the other party and used to request adjustments in the amount of child or spousal support. A new spouse might want to keep his or her tax information out of the picture, and filing separately would achieve that end. Another involves IRS liens on a partner's refund. In general, however, as of this writing, filing separately costs more in taxes because it removes certain tax advantages gained by filing jointly. The rules in this arena are subject to change, so if the amounts involved are significant, check with your accountant.

In general, what are my legal obligations to my spouse?

Your legal and financial obligations to your spouse are exactly the same as your spouse's obligations to you—the law is egalitarian with respect to the marriage contract. According to the statutes in most states, this contract obliges each of you to provide basic financial support to the other. Husband and wife take on what are known as "obligations of mutual respect, fidelity, and support." These include payment for shelter, food, and medical care, and become applicable if a spouse becomes ill or loses—or quits—a job.

What are my legal rights with respect to my spouse?

Again, your legal rights in marriage are exactly the same as your spouse's rights. They include the right to file joint income-tax returns with the IRS and state taxing agencies; to create a "family partnership" under federal tax laws, which allows you to divide business income among family members (often lowering the total tax); to create a marital life estate trust; to receive spouse's and dependents' Social Security, disability, unemployment, veteran's, pension, and public-assistance benefits; to receive a share of your deceased spouse's estate; to claim an estate-tax marital deduction; to receive family rates for insurance; to avoid the deportation of a noncitizen spouse; to enter hospital intensive-care units and other places where visitors are restricted to immediate family; to make medical decisions about your spouse in the event of disability; and to claim the marital communications privilege, which means a court can't force you to disclose the content of conversations between you and your spouse during your marriage.

You mentioned debts earlier. Am I liable for debts my spouse incurred before we got married?

No. You don't marry debt. But as soon as you commingle your assets with your spouse's, any *joint* account you set up becomes fair game for prior creditors. You can get around this law in certain states by keeping or opening a bank account in your own name, which creditors theoretically can't touch. Even so, the IRS has the power to put a lien on a refund due when you file a joint tax return. So your spouse's prior tax liens are the scariest debts to marry.

Am I liable for debts incurred after our marriage that are only in my spouse's name?

You may be. It depends on where you live, but in most states you and your spouse are financially responsible for each other. If your spouse can't pay his debts, creditors will try to force you to pay, and you'll have to go to some lengths (and expense) to prove you're not liable.

What happens if my spouse files for bankruptcy?

If you were legally married when your spouse's debts were incurred, creditors may be able to come after you even after bankruptcy has been filed—even if you two are now divorced. Moreover, if you are both deemed liable for the debt, your spouse's discharge of the debt in bankruptcy court will not relieve you of the debt, which, believe it or not, can show up as a flag on your credit report. The obligation to share in a spouse's debt is a major risk of marriage.

What does the marital contract say about the illness or death of a spouse, and about divorce?

It says a lot. In case of serious illness, the marriage contract gives you the right to make decisions about your spouse's medical care if he or she is not competent to make those decisions. In the case of a spouse's death, the marriage contract may include a legal obligation by your spouse to share his or her estate with you (and vice versa). Many states allow a spouse to take "a forced share," meaning a set amount every spouse is entitled to by law, regardless of a deceased spouse's wishes. The amount varies, but it can be up to one-half of the estate. You have the right to retirement and government benefits based on your spouse's contributions—including disability payments, income from various pensions, and Social Security. In the event of a divorce, you have the right to claim a share of the property and income you and your spouse accumulated during marriage, and in some cases, you may be entitled to half of all combined joint assets.

What about property that I acquired before the marriage? How is this regarded by the courts?

Property acquired before marriage is generally known as separate property. It remains separate for as long as you keep it in your name alone, your spouse doesn't have access to it, and your spouse doesn't contribute to its maintenance. (To be safe, specify your intention to keep your property separate in a pre-nup.) Problems can arise if your partner contributes time and/or money to help maintain a premarital property, thus increasing its value. In some states, whether or not your part-ner makes a contribution of time or money, the appreciation of the property—that is, any increase in value—may be con-sidered a joint asset, unless the pre-nup states otherwise.

What if I owned rental property before I was married and continue to earn money from it during the mar-riage—is the rental income still considered my sepa-rate property?

Good question. In some states, if you and your partner both invest time and effort in the management of the property, the current income may be considered a joint asset. If you use a management company, the rent is more likely to be considered a separate asset. Laws about this vary widely, so check the laws in your state.

What if I'm left an inheritance or given a gift of money by my parents after I'm married? Is that considered joint property?

In most states, the answer is no—*if* the money was given specif-ically to you and you keep it in your name only, or if you buy something with it in your name only. Please note, however, that the longer a marriage goes on, the more the lines blur between partners' separate property. Keeping clear title is crucial.

What about marriage and Social Security? I am a mar-ried woman who works and pays Social Security taxes, but a friend of mine told me she'll be eligible for Social Security benefits based on her husband's work

record, even though she's never worked or paid Social Security taxes. Does this mean that the Social Security taxes I'm paying are wasted, since I could get benefits on my husband's record without ever working?

Your friend is correct. However, the Social Security taxes you are paying are not wasted—not by a long shot. As a married woman who works and pays Social Security taxes, you are eligible for your own retirement benefits. You may get a higher benefit when you retire than you would if your benefit were based solely on your husband's earnings. You may be able to retire before your husband does and receive benefits based on your own earnings. Also, as a working woman, you are eligible to earn disability protection for yourself and your dependent children and, in the event of your death, your survivors may be eligible for benefits based on your earnings.

Both my husband and I work and pay Social Security taxes. On which record will my benefit be based?

You will choose, based on which amount is higher. You are entitled to receive benefits based on your own work record if you have worked long enough to become eligible—usually ten years. However, if the benefits you could receive as a spouse are higher than your own Social Security retirement benefits, you and your spouse will receive a combined benefit based on the higher spouse's benefit.

JOINT ACCOUNTS

Should my wife and I open a joint bank account?

In my opinion, a joint checking account or a money-market fund with both of your names on it is essential. You have decided to join your lives and share your financial resources, and this account is symbolic of that union. Unless you plan to start calculating who drinks more orange juice or uses more toothpaste, you must have a place to house the money you use to pay for your shared bills and expenses. You must also start saving together for the future.

OK, I've done the monthly income-and-expense calculations you suggested earlier. Our expenses, including the additional 10 percent, come to about $4,000 a month. Now what?

Now you and your spouse should prepare to contribute exactly the same *percentage* of your salaries toward the expenses that you share, just as I advise couples who are living together to do. (See page 11.) But remember: The amounts you contribute do not have to be the same to make your contributions equal, only the percentages.

It doesn't seem fair that I have to contribute more just because I make more. Does this mean I have a bigger say in how we spend the money?

On a percentage basis, you are not contributing more; you and your husband are contributing the same *proportion* of your salaries to the joint account. Also, in most states, both parties' income is legally considered joint property, since the marriage is a financial as well as an emotional partnership, remember? Third, even though you may be paid more than your spouse, this does not mean you work harder. Nor should you have more power over your resources or be entitled to a larger voice in decision-making. The world, as most of us discovered when we were children, is seldom a fair place—if it were, women wouldn't make an average $0.74 to every dollar a man makes. The measure of a committed relationship is this and only this: Is each partner bringing all possible resources to the relationship?

If we have a joint checking account, do we need individual checking accounts as well?

Yes. Grown-ups need discretionary income. Sharing is important in a marriage or other committed relationship, but so is autonomy. Consider how you would feel if you had to ask permission to buy a new tie or pair of shoes every time you needed one. That would be stultifying, wouldn't it? Remember that there are three entities here—yours, mine, and the big one, ours. Ours is most important, but yours and mine still count.

My husband has been responsible for making a monthly deposit to our joint checking account for the car payment. Now that the car is paid off, he says he shouldn't have to put that money into the joint account. Do you agree?

No. You and your husband now have a chance to increase your future nest egg—so please don't blow it! When a loan has been paid off or a former expense (day care, for instance) disappears, the amount of money you were paying toward it should continue to be paid at the same interval—into an investment vehicle you choose together, toward a goal you both share.

Once our individual and joint accounts are set up, how do we save for our future together?

The first step is to contribute as much as you can to your employers' 401(k) plans or other work-related retirement plans and/or to an IRA. (If you are self-employed, fund a SEP-IRA or a Keogh plan.) As your circumstances improve, regularly contribute to a non-retirement-plan investment vehicle as well. Once again, use a proportional-contribution approach to creating this nest egg, which you should plan to share equally in the future. If one of you makes considerably more money than the other and wants to invest more than the proportional amount, it is up to both of you to decide—preferably in a pre-nup—to whom that money will go in the event of a divorce.

NET WORTH AND SELF-WORTH

Although my spouse and I contribute proportional amounts of our salaries, my share is smaller, so I feel as if I'm not pulling my weight. What can I do?

In spite of how you may feel at times, the smaller amount you earn does not make you more or less important, deserving, or entitled to participate in decision-making. Many people who do meaningful work, *vital* work, are underpaid—teachers, social workers, stay-at-home moms—while others are paid handsomely for work that in the long run may not make a difference to anyone. Do not—I repeat, do not—value yourself or your partner by income. Begin, and continue, as equals. People first, then money. If this is a problem for either of you, there is emotional work that you need to tackle now!

My partner and I have lived together for about three years, and I have supported her financially during that time. My income is large in comparison to hers, and it seems that this discrepancy has created a chasm between us. She feels she will never be able to match my contributions to the relationship, so what's the point? How can I level the playing field?

Different income levels can become a sticking point in a relationship, but they don't have to be. Money can be one of the most creative forces in the world, as well as one of the most destructive. What's certain is that money is a force we have to reckon with. Those with less money or with simpler possessions than others around them—especially when the others are their partners or spouses—are likely to feel inadequate or intimidated. Finding a solution begins with acknowledging the problem, as you have done.

Then how do we bridge the gap created by our different incomes?

First of all, be extremely careful not to create an environment in which your partner feels that her lack of financial resources is holding you back or keeping you from doing the things you love; that can only add to any feeling she may have that she's less than a full partner, and may also make her feel that she will never have—or be—enough. Keep this in mind before blurting out, "Hey, let's go to Paris for the weekend!" Tailor some of your activities to her resources. Try eating at home or in restaurants that she can afford, too. It is very important that she be able to carry her own weight when it comes to money. Otherwise, before you know it, she'll feel powerless, which leads to feeling resentful.

Second, I want you to examine your own heart. Deep down, do you feel your partner is worth less because she makes less? If so, is there anything that you can do to help her make more? Ask yourself what you believe makes for true equality and where equality lies. In a bankbook? In your bedroom? In your heart? Once you've examined yourself, talk with your partner about her perceptions of your different financial capabilities. Be as honest, supportive, and reassuring as you can be.

If your partner were to ask me for advice, I would say this: Recognize that gifts of the heart are priceless. Your boyfriend may be able to buy anything he wants for himself, but he can't buy you and he can't buy love. What you bring to this relationship has great value that has nothing to do with money. You do, however, have to be strong and not overextend yourself financially just to keep up with him. You have to pay your own way when you can, and know when to draw the line when it comes to matching your partner's spending.

I make very little money, but my spouse makes a lot—and says it's OK if I use my money for my own needs and don't contribute to the joint household bills. Will this work?

In my opinion, this won't work—in fact, chances are that as the years go by, it will backfire. When one person pays for everything, what usually happens is that he or she slowly begins to feel a sense of ownership toward everything, as well as a creeping resentment toward the person who is not paying his or her way. What's more, the person who is not making a financial contribution gradually feels less powerful, more dependent, and less entitled to participate in joint financial decisions, which is each partner's right in a committed relationship. If you are working, it would be best for you to contribute an equal percentage, even if that means you pay just a few dollars a month. In a shared life, you *both* have to pay.

What if I would like to stop working for money and stay home to take care of the children?

The first thing to ask yourself is this: Is staying at home financially feasible? To answer this question, I recommend that you and your spouse add up all your expenses—everything from the mortgage to food, clothes, and schooling for your children. (If you are paying for day care, you can reclaim those costs.) Now, how much of your spouse's income would be left over each month if you stopped working? If there would be little or nothing left, and you both decide that this is the right course to follow, then you must share equally in the responsibility of caring for your money. If there *is* some discretionary money, it should be split fifty-fifty, regardless of who's bringing it in. Remember, in most states, all married couples' income is considered to be jointly owned, and that should be the guiding principle of your partnership.

If I do decide to stay home with the children, how do we live on one income?

There is no simple formula for "finding" the money in this situation. You and your spouse must work together to adjust the variables, whether it means seeking a higher-paying job for the partner who earns more money, moving to a more affordable house or apartment, or learning to make do without certain luxuries.

Once we've figured out the financial side of my staying home with the children, what else should my spouse and I think about?

After you've worked out the finances, the most important thing is that you and your spouse agree that it's desirable for you to stay home with the children. Resentment on either side is a pretty clear indicator that the arrangement won't work. You must agree, too, that any assets accumulated belong to both of you, not solely to the partner earning money. And you must find a way to ensure that you both keep in mind that the partner who is staying home is a full, equal partner with equal rights and isn't subtly belittled. After all, the stay-home partner will be doing work equal to, if not more important than, that of the partner who marches off in a gray suit to the office every morning.

Both my husband and I go to an office every day. What if one of us loses our job?

If your relationship is strong and you've talked about this contingency beforehand, you'll get through the crisis. Remember the extra 10 percent I asked you to put into your joint fund every month? This is one of the things it's designed for; it's there to help you both in times of trouble. Handling setbacks together is part of the challenge and joy of marriage.

DEALING WITH
PREVIOUS MARRIAGES

The man I'm about to marry has an ex-wife and two children, whom he still supports. Will my income be considered by the court when it is deciding how much his alimony and child support payments will be?

Technically, no, it will not. However, if the ex-wife petitions the court for increased payments, the court will look at your joint household income and expenses. If your spouse has more disposable income because you and he have combined incomes, then your non-parental income has essentially entered the picture. Your income may be exempt from consideration if you and your husband keep your money separate, although in some states your income-tax returns can be subpoenaed to find out your combined household income before setting (or changing) the amount of your husband's payments.

Are these payments tax-deductible?

Typically, alimony payments are tax-deductible to the person who makes the payments but taxable to the recipient; child-support payments are generally tax-free but not tax-deductible.

If my ex-spouse doesn't pay child support, can the court still enforce her visitation rights?
Yes. Financial and custodial arrangements are considered by courts to be distinct and separate issues.

How can I keep from feeling resentful of the time and money my spouse spends on his previous family? What's legitimate, and what's too much?
How much time your spouse spends with his or her ex-wife and children is a matter that must, in the end, be decided by him or her. No formula applies. "Blood is thicker than water"— or time, or money—is a principle that operates when considering past obligations as well as current ones. Try to look at your spouse's emotional and financial commitment to a former family as a mark of personal honor that promises security to you as well as to them. Still, if you feel left out or overlooked, calmly talk to your spouse about your feelings—taking care to talk *to*, not *at*, your spouse. Make an effort to view this former family as an extension of your new family; otherwise, you risk losing access to the part of your spouse that cares for them. Don't cut off a part of him or her from you.

SEPARATION

How is separation different from divorce?
Separation gives both partners the opportunity to find out what it would be like to live apart from each other—in separate residences and often with separate finances. In some states, you can file for legal separation only as a prelude to divorce. In other states, you can be separated indefinitely, without ever getting a divorce. Basically, legal separation is

defined as no longer living together and not having the intention to reconcile. It is a kind of limbo, since one of you has probably moved out, but you are still legally married and cannot marry another person.

What is an informal separation?

An informal separation is simply a way of saying that one of you has moved out, often to give one or both of you time to think things over. Though you may eventually get a divorce, this is not necessarily the intention of either of you when you informally separate. In some cases, you may not *want* a divorce, perhaps for religious, financial, or practical reasons, such as the maintenance of your health insurance coverage. Note that in an informal separation, you may both have the same legal responsibilities and duties to each other as you did when you were living together.

Then what is a legal separation?

In some states, moving out with no intention of returning *constitutes* a legal separation, which can fix the date for certain financial matters. (Before separating, check with an attorney or your state attorney general's office to see whether this applies in your state.) When your separation is a conscious first step toward filing for divorce, you and/or your spouse can apply for a formal legal separation. Before filing a petition for separation with the county court, ask your attorney to prepare a legal separation agreement or to look over an agreement that you and your spouse have drafted together.

Is one type of separation better than the other?

A lot depends on the intentions of the parties involved. A formal separation agreement obviously spells out legal and financial matters much more clearly than an informal separation does. Therefore, a formal separation guarantees greater certainty. For example, it can state whether your spouse will support you financially during the period when you are living apart. If you have children together, it can detail visitation and support arrangements. It can specify how you will divide the property that you share. This diminishes the potential for misunderstandings and strife, and if you do end up getting a divorce, a lot of things will have already been set down on paper.

Why is the date that you agree to separate important?
Depending on the state in which you live, the date of separation can matter a great deal in determining the financial outcome in a divorce or legal separation. Among other issues, it can affect how much alimony may be at stake, your responsibility for any debt incurred by your spouse before and after the date of separation, and how you'll divide retirement assets (though not your right to a share of your spouse's Social Security benefits, which is based on the date of divorce).

If you know or sense that you may be headed for divorce, try to plan your separation date with all these factors in mind. To take just one example, I learned firsthand how important setting the separation date can be when the husband of a very good friend of mine came home and announced, apparently out of the clear blue sky, that he wanted a divorce. He asked my friend to move out as soon as possible. I couldn't figure out what had happened and why it was so sudden and urgent. A few days later, as my friend was preparing to move, I happened to read that the company her husband was working for had just been bought out and that in two months' time all employees were going to receive generous stock options and a pension plan. My friend's husband knew that if this took place after he and his wife were officially separated, there was a good chance that he wouldn't have to share this windfall with her. It was a tense two months, but she waited them out before taking any action to separate, which was a very smart move on her part.

Why do people separate in the first place? Shouldn't they just make up their minds to get a divorce or not get a divorce?

Couples have many reasons for agreeing to separate. Some want to find out what living apart feels like. Others need time and solitude to analyze the relationship—what is right about it as well as what is wrong. If you are married to someone who has shown problematic behavior (for example, excessive drinking, infidelity, or verbal or physical abuse), separating shows that you are dead serious about asking that person to change or else. Or you may know that you want a divorce and can't bear the thought of living with your spouse until the divorce is official. Or you may have religious or financial reasons for staying married for a little while longer. Finally, you may live in a state where you have to be legally separated before you can file for divorce.

Can I throw my spouse out of the house, especially if I owned the house before we got married?

It is a staple of state law that neither spouse can be excluded from the other's dwelling. If a domestic situation becomes violent, barring the violent partner from the house requires a court-issued restraining order.

Can I "date" my husband while the two of us are separated?

My advice would be to consult your attorney before you consider dating your spouse during a separation. A lot depends on whether you have filed (or are planning to file) for a divorce in which one of you is at fault. Imagine, for example, that you separate from your husband and file for a divorce from him on the grounds of mental cruelty, then date him again to see if your relationship can be rekindled. If the reconciliation doesn't work out, the court isn't likely to take your complaint of mental cruelty very seriously. (Some states, however, are "no fault," and no evidence of mental cruelty or infidelity needs to be shown—only that "irreconcilable differences" arose.)

But what if my spouse and I intend to reconcile somewhere along the line?

Again, I would consult your attorney. In general, if you and your spouse are planning to reconcile, I don't see a problem in your sharing a pizza.

What is the downside of separating from my spouse?

In many cases, the downside is financial. You may have come to rely on your spouse's income, and without it your expenses will seem outsized. In the worst-case scenario, you may be cut off from the prospective income of your spouse and may not have enough money to rent or buy a new residence and support yourself. Finally, remember that even though you are living apart, you and your spouse are still married and therefore still responsible for each other's debts.

How do things stand legally if I tell my spouse I want to separate? And what if I move out?

It depends. In some states, if you want to separate but your husband doesn't, moving out may unwittingly give your husband grounds for a fault divorce. In some states you can be charged with desertion if you separate informally.

Is there any way I can protect myself legally?

Yes. Make sure that all these issues are covered and very carefully worded in a separation agreement that you work out with your spouse and your respective attorneys.

My husband and I have just agreed to a separation. Where should I concentrate my efforts, money-wise?

Once a separation seems inevitable, you must turn your attention to financial matters as quickly as you can. If you procrastinate, you may one day find that you are responsible for credit card debt that was incurred right after you moved out, or that one of your joint accounts has been wiped clean of its assets, or that the home equity line of credit that was there in case of emergencies now has a loan against it for $20,000, for which you are responsible. Do not be afraid to separate your accounts immediately. If you end up getting back together, you can always reopen those accounts.

In specific financial terms, what exactly should I do?

What follows is an overview of everything that should be done immediately after it becomes clear that a separation is imminent.

- Consult an attorney regarding the divorce laws in your particular state, and their applicability to your particular situation.
- If you don't already have a checking account in your name only, open one.
- Close all joint accounts, including credit card accounts. Don't freeze money accounts, because one or both of you may need access to the funds. With your attorneys' approval, split the money from joint accounts equally.
- Make copies of all financial documents that show your

true debts, assets, and expenses, including tax returns, bank records, household and credit card bills, records of expenses for the children, and any records of every penny you spend to live from month to month.

- Start keeping track of all debts incurred and money paid to each other after the date of separation. This includes money spent on joint bills, improvements to the home, moving expenses, children, insurance premiums—everything that pertains to the two of you. If you decide to pay support to your spouse while you are working things out, make sure that all these sums are documented and that you have an agreement in writing as to what these funds are to go for. If you have such an agreement, these payments may be tax-deductible, although they will be considered taxable income to your spouse.

- See a tax specialist to decide whether you are going to file your tax return jointly or separately.

- Sit down and figure out what you are worth as a couple. First determine the value of everything you own jointly. Gather documentation of all your joint assets— your home or homes, real estate, jewelry, art, furnishings, automobiles, investments, retirement plans, bonds, mutual funds, savings or money-market accounts, etc. In addition, consider a tricky and relatively new area, stock options, which give an employee the right to buy a company's stock at a great discount but often may not be exercised for years after they are issued. If your spouse has stock options, see an attorney at once, as most states are still sorting out whether, in a divorce, a stock option that may not be exercised until years after the divorce should be considered a joint asset at the time of divorce.

- After you determine what you have in assets, as well as your expenses and income, try to work out an equitable division. Don't do this before you have all the relevant information and documentation, however, because you can't negotiate without the facts. Finally, don't agree to anything without consulting an attorney and a tax specialist.
- Reduce your spending wherever possible to generate some savings for the rocky road ahead.

What about debt? Once we are separated, am I still responsible for any and all debts that my spouse incurs?

In most scenarios, the official date of separation in a final judgment or decree officially determines when you are no longer responsible for any new debts that your spouse incurs in his or her name alone. That's one reason to make sure all joint credit card accounts are closed when you separate. Make sure, too, that you divide all debts and know who is responsible for each one. Before doing so, set up a credit card account in your name to make sure that you qualify for credit, since sometimes your individual credit rating can be affected when you close out a credit card account. Also, contact all professionals and service providers (doctors, lawyers, dentists, etc.) and inform them in writing that if any work is being done for your spouse, you will not be responsible for the bills. The IRS has recently loosened its rules regarding "innocent spouses," making it easier to disavow the income-tax obligations of an ex-spouse, so be sure to check with your accountant about any potential tax liabilities. Even if all these precautions are taken, it's still possible that creditors might come after you, seeking payment for bills your spouse incurred. Thus the more accounts you can close, the better off you are. Note, too, that under the "obligations of mutual respect, fidelity, and support" clause of the marital contract, you may still be held responsible for debts your spouse runs up for the necessities of life during the separation period and before any divorce is final. Necessities of life include housing, food, clothes, children's expenses, and medical expenses.

Please note that, for many people, the hardest part of separation or divorce is money. People can move away from each other and start new lives, either temporarily or permanently, but they often seem unable to cut financial ties as cleanly—this is particularly true when minor children are involved. Sometimes letting go of jointly managed money seems like the ultimate move, and they're not ready to do that yet. For other couples, living in two places increases their costs of living and may force them to sell their house and other assets. In other cases, guilt keeps the money together. Or the person who has always handled the money keeps handling it because it's familiar and easy, or because both parties are simply too lazy to separate the funds. But whatever the reason, it is a mistake to remain financially intimate after you have severed domestic and emotional ties.

Why is financial intimacy bad if my spouse and I are separated?

I have seen it time and time again: When a spouse continues to foot the bills after a separation, resentment builds up on one side and an unhealthy dependence is created on the other. Having one spouse continue to make a house payment for a brief period so that you can avoid having to sell your house suddenly and ill-advisedly, for example, is certainly worth considering, but don't wait too long to separate your financial lives. Otherwise, mutual respect and individual financial power will go out the window.

If you decide to pay for items for your spouse after you have separated, it is very important to set a time limit. Establish a start and a stop date. Put this in writing, so that there is no misunderstanding. Remember, when one person is in shock—usually the person who is being left—he or she is not going to hear things accurately or remember them clearly. Do not set yourself or your spouse up for additional misunderstandings or disappointments. With your attorneys' help, put *all* your temporary arrangements in writing. Both of you should sign this and keep a copy.

If my spouse and I have been separated for a long time and I haven't been working, can I collect any of his Social Security benefits?

Not according to the rules of the Social Security Administration, which pays benefits only to the main beneficiary—in this case, your spouse—once he or she reaches retirement age and applies to collect them, *unless* you are divorced from your spouse. As far as the SSA is concerned, a marriage is a marriage until it is legally dissolved. If you live in Kansas and your spouse lives in Texas, and you haven't spoken for five years, but neither of you has gotten around to dissolving your marriage, then in the eyes of the SSA you are still legally married and therefore you are not eligible for your own benefits based on your spouse's work record. However, if you've been married for at least ten years, you may be eligible for dependents benefits. The bottom line is, if you are close to the ten-year mark, wait until you have passed it to get a legal divorce so that you can qualify for Social Security on your spouse's record. However, in order to collect, you must be divorced.

What are the presumptions of the court with respect to custody of children?

Courts in most states believe that joint legal custody is best for children and encourage joint physical custody as well. They will not award sole custody to a parent unless there's a strong showing of proof of the unfitness of the other parent. But courts in some states will not award joint custody unless both parties agree to it. Incidentally, this is one issue that can't be predisposed of in a prenuptial agreement.

Who is responsible for an incapacitated child?

The father and mother share equal responsibility for an incapacitated or disabled child. In most states, when the child turns 18, he or she is considered a conservatee (the age may vary from state to state); the parents become the child's conservators and manage any state or federal money for which the child is eligible. In turn, the state may access money that you or your spouse have put aside to be held for the benefit of the child. If you have a child (or, for that matter, a parent) who will need long-term assistance, please see a good trust lawyer who deals with asset protection.

THE EMOTIONS OF DIVORCE

To my great disappointment, my marriage hasn't worked out, and my husband and I have decided to split up. I never thought this would happen, and I alternate between fear and outright panic. What should I be thinking about?

First, be assured that you will get through this, just as you have gotten through other difficulties in your life. How well you get through it will largely be determined by whether you reach for your courage or turn away from it, toward feelings of pain and helplessness. During this transition period, you are going to have to make quite a few decisions, and it is vital that, when you do so, your mind and body be as strong as possible. Act with strength, which will create more strength. Eat well, exercise, and allow yourself plenty of sleep. Consider counseling or a support group for you and your children. Even if the motions feel hollow at first, the actions are powerful and will nourish your courage.

It is also important for you to remember that when you got married, you and your mate gave your word that you would honor each other for better or for worse, forever. Now that you are facing a divorce, you are breaking that vow in the practical realm, but you must still honor the "for worse" part of that promise on an emotional level—if only for your own sake. Your thoughts, your words, and every single action you take at this time will govern your future and give you control over it.

How can my thoughts and words give me control over my future?

I'm a firm believer that your thoughts and your words create your destiny. One of my favorite books is a tenth-century Hindu text called *The Outlook of Shiva,* written by a scholar named Somananda. In it, Somananda instructs us to act as if we already embody our goal, no matter how large the disparity between what we are and how we feel now, and what we wish to become or achieve. It is important for us not to allow doubt, sadness, anger, or confusion to cause us to abandon our intention. Instead, we must begin by clarifying our highest and noblest goals, and then we should try to maintain "an unwavering awareness" by affirming these goals with confidence and conviction. In this way, Somananda explains, our being aligns itself with our intention, and our goal becomes manifest. In short, become it by thinking it. Be it by saying it.

Sometimes I feel as if going through the death of some-
body I love would be less difficult than a divorce.

You're not alone. Over the years, I have come to believe that a
death—whether foreseeable or unexpected—is in some ways
easier to cope with than a divorce. With death there usually is
no blame. Everybody suffers loss—the person who's died and
the loved ones left behind. A life is gone. The community
gathers around you in mourning. Friends and relatives, some
of whom you may not have seen in years, check in to see how
you are doing. If you have children, they draw closer to you.
There is usually not much ambiguity, emotional or financial.
The house is yours to sell or keep as you see fit, the car is yours,
the retirement account, the life insurance policy, the possessions—everything that was "ours" is now yours. When someone you love dies, the loss is enormous, to be sure. But you
don't lose the love, which remains pure.

So in emotional as well as financial terms, divorce is
actually very different from experiencing the death of
a loved one?

Yes. If you are the bereaved party in the event of a divorce,
you may be faced with an ex-partner who is living a perfectly
happy life, perhaps with somebody else. You may feel that for
all you gave to the relationship, you got little back in return.
You may also be filled with regrets about how you behaved,
fearing that you may have forced your partner to leave you.
Perhaps you are making do with less while your former partner is
living on more. If you have children, your former partner may
take them away from you one or two nights a week and every
other weekend and show them a great time. The children
themselves are likely to be as confused and angry as you are.
As for the community, not everyone is rallying around you
unconditionally, the way they probably would have if your

spouse had died; no one's dropping off supper for you, and the phone is hardly ringing off the hook. Instead, some of your friends may feel uncomfortable around you. In fact, some of them may be taking your ex-spouse's side, compounding your loss. To rebuild your life from this point of disequilibrium will take enormous courage.

I am so full of hatred toward the person who came between my husband and me that I don't know what to do!

Of course you feel this way, especially if you're being left for someone else—even if you recognize that the person who takes this role rarely comes uninvited. Nevertheless, if all your energies are devoted to hatred or revenge, you won't have a whole lot left for more constructive pursuits. If you think about this hatred all the time, then you'll talk about it and act on it, and you will be building a hateful, vengeful foundation on which to live the rest of your life. Try to pull away from the hatred as much as you can and instead expend your energies on caring for yourself. If you're really having difficulty, check out anger-management classes offered in your area.

How can I even begin to cope with the emotions of separation and divorce?

As I said, a good place to start is by remembering that every action you take today will have an effect tomorrow. Are you saying to yourself, "I've never been so angry in my life"? If you are, you should keep in mind that acting from anger not only threatens to impair your good judgment when it comes to making vital decisions, it can also increase your attorneys' fees. You're better off paying a therapist, who charges a lot less, than paying an attorney to listen to your emotional issues. What usually happens to people who angrily refuse to settle with their partners is that they end up spending a lot more time in conflict—and paying more money as a result.

So anger has a financial as well as an emotional cost. Just how much more does it cost not to settle or compromise?

On average, a divorce trial in court can cost up to three times as much as an out-of-court settlement, and that's just money. The emotional costs also can be huge.

Are you saying that I shouldn't take my divorce to trial even if my ex-spouse is being completely unreasonable?

No. If your estranged spouse is being unreasonable and there seems to be no amicable way to resolve your differences, do not be afraid to go to court to have the judge determine the final accounting, assign responsibility for any debts, divide any remaining assets, and settle issues of child and spousal support, attorneys' fees, and so on. Sometimes it is better to have a rational judge decide your fate than to let your angry spouse (or your angry self!) call the shots. You must do this, however, with eyes that are open, unclouded by any toxic emotions that can prevent you from seeing plain facts or probable outcomes.

In addition to anger, what are some other reactions people have when they are facing a divorce?

One common reaction is to insist that you don't care about the outcome of the divorce or about what happens to your ex-spouse or to yourself. "I just want to get all this behind me and get on with my life," people say. There are other destructive phrases that I hear, too. "I don't want anything. He [or she] can have it all." Or "I'm not worried about the money. I know he [or she] will be fair." None of the above is an advisable attitude or belief. Anger and revenge will get you nowhere fast, but so will the martyr approach, in which you throw up your hands and let your spouse have everything. This makes little emotional or financial sense. You were half of your marriage, after all. As for believing that your estranged spouse will continue to be fair to you because he or she has been fair up to this point, well, when it comes to dividing assets—which means giving up money—people can behave very strangely, and someone you once thought of as the most generous person in the world may surprise, appall, and disappoint you.

If you find yourself thinking or saying any of the phrases above, I want to ask you: Are you still being mindful of the awesome power of words? Do you know that when you say you don't care what happens, you are in effect creating a situation that almost surely will prevent you from getting on with your life in a conscious, rich, and productive way? Remember, you may spend many more years divorced from your spouse than you spent married to him or her; therefore, the decisions you make during this crucial time will affect you (and perhaps your children) for many years to come. Do not take casually what is happening to you right now. Divorce is as serious a commitment to the future as marriage was. Now is the time I want you to summon words of wealth.

What do you mean by "words of wealth"?

Words of wealth are words like these: "I want to get on with my life, but I care deeply about what happens now, because what happens now will affect me and possibly my children forever." You must be mindful of the present tense, and also keep in mind how swiftly the future becomes the present. And the future may not involve just you, but also your children and their children. Say the words of wealth to your attorney and to your ex, and say them with grace until they become true.

I don't really care about the money—I just want my wife back!

So often when divorce is imminent, the person who is being left finds it very hard to face what is happening. He or she starts thinking or saying things like, "I can get her back if I do whatever she wants." But you are not one iota likelier to save your marriage by downplaying the importance of money or giving up your rights to it. All you are likely to do with this kind of thinking is impoverish your future, financially *and* emotionally. With thoughts and words like the ones above, you are about to serve yourself a double whammy. Not only will you repel money, money that is rightfully yours, but the person you are trying to bring closer will be repelled, too—by your lack of self-respect and your powerlessness. No one is attracted to weakness. Maybe you can put your marriage back together, maybe not. But please don't base your financial actions (or, for that matter, your emotional actions) on an unproved possibility. Protecting yourself will have absolutely no effect on a possible reconciliation, I can promise you that. If anything, your actions now—strong, powerful, clear, grace-ful, and rich—will better the chances for a reconciliation.

And in the meantime, you're telling me to be very watch-ful of my feelings, day in and day out.

Yes. Count on feeling fine one day, and the next day feeling wretched. On the days when the blues hit you big-time, give yourself permission to take a break. Try not to make any deci-sions if you don't have to. For the first six months after your breakup, rate yourself on a scale of one to ten twice a day—when you get up and about eight hours later—a one rating being extremely happy and ten being miserable. If ever you feel you are a five or more, please do not make any decisions regarding your money or your divorce on that day. If you are asked to, simply say, "Not today, thank you," let it go at that, and address the matter when you feel better. Remember, check yourself *twice* a day, because sometimes a phone call, a song on the radio, a comment from a friend, or even two people walking down the street holding hands can set off a chain of emotions that transform a one into an eight before you know what hit you. "Not today, thank you" is an expression of self-respect, coming from a position of power.

I am the person who was left. What angers me most is that my ex-husband seems to be doing so much better than I am. How can I get myself to start doing as well as he seems to be?

Please realize that you are not in a contest to see who can get through this divorce with the fewest breakdowns or, for that matter, the fewest feelings. If you are the one who was left, do not be surprised if your spouse seems to be doing better than you are. Try to be glad your spouse is thriving, as this will certainly make your life easier! Remember that the chances are pretty good that he or she has been thinking about this divorce for a long time, long enough to get used to the idea, whereas for you it is brand-new and devastating. Your job now is to rebuild your life by identifying and then acting in your own best interests.

Do not get pushed into doing anything during this difficult time. Start using your daily ratings immediately and take action only when you feel ready. You have the power to set the pace of the divorce. You have the power, too, to drag it out, but that won't help you. Use your power wisely, and proceed when you are ready. I urge you also to seek therapy or counseling if you can possibly afford it and/or to consult a member of the clergy. Though it's very helpful to receive sympathy and emotional support from family and friends, if you let them see you at your lowest point too often, it may be hard to restore equilibrium to your relationships later, when you feel stronger. You don't want friends to treat you like a victim for the rest of your life, do you? Plus, you may need assistance beyond sympathy. A professional counselor's impartiality may help make you stronger, both in the short and long term. (Take care in choosing one: As in every profession, there are good practitioners, and less good ones. Ask around.) If there are children involved, a counselor may also help you in dealing with their pain and confusion and in deciding whether they, too, need professional help.

I left my wife and now I am overcome by all sorts of emotions that I find it hard to live with. Any advice?
For the person who leaves, the responsibilities are immense. Regardless of your feelings today, you have just delivered a terrible blow to the person who was once the love of your life. For your own benefit as well as your ex-spouse's, I want you to proceed slowly and with compassion. Your marriage didn't work out. Now it is your responsibility to conclude it as successfully as possible. How you end something as profound and important as a marriage is a reflection of how you live your life—financially, emotionally, and spiritually.

ANNULMENTS

I am a practicing Roman Catholic, and I am wondering if instead of a separation and a divorce I can get my five-year marriage annulled.
There are two different kinds of annulments, a legal annulment and a religious annulment. The latter is associated with

the Catholic Church and doesn't eliminate the need for a divorce. If you are Catholic and you do divorce and wish to marry someone else, the church will not formally recognize your new marriage until your old marriage is annulled.

How do I go about getting a religious annulment?

If you are a divorced Roman Catholic and you want to remarry under the auspices of that church, you should first make an appointment to see your parish priest. Next, a church court, known as a marriage tribunal, meets to discuss all the elements of your previous marriage, including the reasons leading to the divorce. During this meeting, the tribunal may ask you to provide a list of friends and family members who were "witnesses" to your marriage, as well as certain legal documents pertaining to your marriage, such as your marriage license.

Will the church contact my ex-husband?

Yes, it will. He will be notified by the marriage tribunal that you want your marriage to be annulled. He then has the right to show the tribunal proof that your marriage was valid. Next the tribunal will review all the evidence, written and oral, and decide whether or not, according to the policies of the Catholic Church, you have grounds for an annulment. If they say no, you have the right to appeal. If you lose your appeal, you can take your request for annulment all the way to Rome!

How long does a church annulment take?

Anywhere from several months to several years.

You mentioned a legal annulment. How does this work?

A legal annulment is a court order that basically announces to the world that your marriage was never legally valid to begin with—it's as though your marriage never took place.

But my marriage did take place! Why would a court declare it invalid?

The most common reason that a court would be willing to declare an annulment is that one spouse lied to, defrauded, or misled the other. The assumption is that if the spouse who was lied to had known the truth, he or she would not have gotten married. Other reasons include a bigamous marriage (one in which your partner was already married), a marriage in which one of the parties wasn't of legal age, a marriage in which one of you was forced into wedlock, or a marriage that took place while one, or both, of you was intoxicated or under the influence of drugs.

Are legal annulments available in all states, or just a few?

Legal annulments are available in most states. Remember, though, that if you and your partner have children, an annulment will not have any effect—nor should it—on your responsibilities as a parent.

DIVORCE

Why are so many people getting divorced these days? It wasn't always that way, was it?

No, it wasn't. For whatever reason—changing values, sexual and women's liberation, or a generation that has different expectations of what a marriage should be and is less willing to "stick it out"—the fact is that these days, one in two marriages ends in divorce. Of the 50 states, Nevada ranks first with the highest divorce rate, and Massachusetts brings up the rear.

How much does it cost to get a divorce?

That depends on a lot of factors, the most important being whether your divorce is amicable, or whether you and your spouse are willing to fight it out to the bitter end. You can get divorced for a few hundred dollars or a few thousand dollars, or you can go all out and spend a small fortune litigating a long divorce trial in court. No matter what state you live in, a pretty good rule of thumb is that the more issues you and your spouse can agree on, the less you will spend on attorneys' fees. Also, obviously, the more experienced or well known the attorney you retain, the greater his or her hourly rate will be. An experienced lawyer, however, may be able to accomplish more in less time.

Can I shop around for an attorney on the basis of cost?

Yes. Many divorce lawyers offer a free brief consultation. Request estimates based on several possible divorce scenarios, including an amicable divorce and a hostile divorce. These will only be approximations, of course, but they will still give you a pretty good idea of how much a divorce will cost you in the end. Interviewing a cross section of lawyers is a good idea for another reason, too: One attorney may tell you that the things you want from your divorce are impossible to get; another attorney may promise you the moon but disappoint you in the end. Consulting with several can help give you a good grounding in what is possible, as well as which attorney you will feel most comfortable with.

So how do I find a really good divorce attorney?

Don't just let your fingers do the walking through the Yellow Pages. Get referrals from friends who have been in the same boat. A shrewd, experienced attorney is essential, particularly if your divorce proceedings promise to be bitter or drawn out.

If this is the case, you should try to find someone who has had extensive courtroom experience. In general, you should be conscious of whether you want a conciliator or a gladiator, and, in either case, make it a priority to find an attorney who is experienced in family law. He or she should be someone with whom you feel very comfortable, though it is also important to remember that your attorney is not your best friend or your confidant, but your lawyer and advocate.

Are there any resources other than referrals for finding a good divorce lawyer?

Yes. Go to your public library and see if it has a copy of the Martindale-Hubbell directory, which lists and evaluates lawyers state by state, city by city. Or call the American Academy of Matrimonial Lawyers at (312) 263-6477, or log on to its website, *www.aaml.org*. Your local bar association may also be a good resource.

I am about to meet with my divorce attorney. What should I bring with me?

Bring the complete list of joint assets that you prepared at the time of separation. You should also bring an inventory of your outstanding debt, whether it's credit card debt, a mortgage, or a student loan. And if you are looking for spousal or child support, you need to know your typical monthly budget and both of your incomes.

My husband and I have been separated for a year. I've retained an attorney and have made a list of all my assets and liabilities. How do I go about filing for divorce?

During the separation, one of you will file a petition for divorce or a complaint in the appropriate court in your or your spouse's county of residence (the name of the court varies from state to state), and this will start the formal divorce proceedings. If you do the filing, you are considered the plaintiff, or the petitioner. Your spouse is considered the defendant, or the respondent. There is no legal preference given to the party that files first.

What goes into a petition for divorce?

Your petition simply puts forth the facts of when you were married, when you separated, your key financial assets and debts, and the number of children who will be affected by the divorce. It also indicates what you want from your spouse, whether it's spousal support, child support, custody of the children, etc.

Does my spouse get a copy of this petition?

After you file your petition, your spouse must be notified and acknowledge formally that you have filed. He may sign what is called a waiver of service, which basically means that he will not be served formally by a process server. This usually happens if a couple has agreed to divorce amicably. If the opposite is true, then your spouse will be served by a process server.

What if for some reason my spouse can't be served—if I don't know where he is, for example? Does this mean we have to stay married forever?

Don't worry, the answer is no. In most states, you can publish a legal notice in your local paper informing your spouse that you have filed a petition for divorce. If after a certain amount of time your spouse fails to come forth, you can obtain a divorce even if your ex doesn't file court papers.

We have two children together. What about them?

If there are children involved, this is the time when one of you may need to file a request for temporary child and spousal support, and for custody, visitation rights, or alimony—or anything else that may apply to your situation—with the local court handling your divorce. You will receive from the court a temporary order soon after this filing, and a permanent order once the divorce is final. Even after that, the court has the right to alter child-support provisions until the children are emancipated, i.e., until they turn 18 or graduate from high school; thus either ex-spouse can petition the court for a change in support payments or custody arrangements until the children become legal adults. The court also retains jurisdiction over spousal support until it is terminated.

Can child-support obligations stop before my child turns 18?

Yes, if your child goes into the military, if he or she takes on a full-time permanent job, if he or she gets married, if he or she becomes legally emancipated, or if he or she dies.

I am paying my wife child support for our three children. Are these payments considered tax-deductible by the IRS?

No. Similarly, if you are a child receiving child support, it is not considered taxable income by the IRS.

What comes after the temporary order?

Next comes the process known as legal discovery—informal or formal—which determines exactly what assets must be divided. If you have children, this information will be used to calculate the amount of child support or alimony that you will have to pay or that you will receive.

What's the difference between informal and formal discovery?

Informal discovery is when your attorney asks your spouse's attorney for information, whether financial, legal, or medical, and your spouse is willing to answer each question honestly and to the best of his ability. Basically, he voluntarily discloses the information that your attorney requires. Formal discovery becomes necessary if your spouse will not provide information needed by your attorney. It involves subpoenas for documents, written interrogatories, and oral depositions under oath.

How long does the discovery process take?

It can take anywhere from a week or two up to several months, depending on whether or not you and your spouse agree on things.

My attorney told me that I am going to be deposed. What should I keep in mind during the deposition process?

A deposition can be nerve-racking, so try to keep calm. Answer all questions truthfully, no matter how painful that may be, but at the same time be very careful about what you say. Try to keep your answers brief and factual, and do not stray from the question that's being asked. If you give more information than is asked for, you may inadvertently harm your case.

What if my spouse refuses to be deposed?

You can request a court order requiring him to appear at a deposition. If your spouse violates the court order, he will risk being held in contempt of court, which might lead to the judge's immediately ruling in your favor.

DIVIDING ASSETS IN DIVORCE

I dread dividing up the assets from our 14-year marriage. How do courts and attorneys go about deciding who gets what?

It is common for a divorcing couple to make decisions about dividing their property and debts themselves rather than leave it to a judge. But if a couple cannot agree, they can submit their property dispute to the court, which will use state law to divide the property.

If this is your case, let me start by saying that an attorney who deals with family issues and divorce sits in the suite next to my office. Her rule-of-thumb advice is to choose your battles carefully. If there is a lot of property to be divided, I advise you to concede gracefully on the smaller stuff, and you'll be on higher ground when it comes to the items that really matter. In short, it's not worth fighting over who gets the orange towels.

In general, the court system is in place to see to the division of property and debts and to settle issues of spousal support, child support, custody, and visitation. In community-property states, everything is divided fifty-fifty, but in other states, the judge has wide discretion to divide assets and debts and to fix spousal support based on equitable principles of need.

How, exactly, do the states differ when dividing property at divorce? Are there major differences between community-property and equitable-distribution states?

Yes, there are important differences. But nowhere does division of property necessarily mean a physical division. Rather, in every state the court awards each spouse a percentage of the total value of the property. (It is illegal for either spouse to hide assets in order to shield them from property division.) Each spouse gets items whose worth adds up to his or her percentage.

States divide property under one of the two schemes you mentioned: equitable distribution or community property.

- Equitable distribution: Assets and earnings accumulated during marriage are divided equitably (fairly), which allows a judge enormous discretion in the event that the parties don't settle. Equitable distribution principles are followed everywhere except in the community-property states listed just below.
- Community property: In Arizona, California, Idaho, Louisiana, Nevada, New Mexico, Texas, Washington, and Wisconsin, all property of married people is classified as either community property, owned equally by both spouses, or the separate property of one spouse. At divorce, community property is generally divided equally between the spouses, while each spouse keeps his or her separate property.

How do we distinguish between community and separate property?

Very generally, here are the rules for determining what's community property and what isn't:

- Community property includes all earnings during marriage and everything acquired with those earnings. All debts incurred during marriage, unless the creditor was specifically looking to the separate property of one spouse for payment, are community-property debts.
- Separate property of one spouse includes assets and debts acquired before marriage or after separation, as well as

gifts and inheritances given just to that spouse, and the proceeds of a pension that vested (that is, the pensioner became legally entitled to receive it) before marriage. Property purchased with the separate funds of a spouse remain that spouse's separate property. A business owned by one spouse before the marriage remains his or her separate property during the marriage, although a portion of it may be considered community property if the business has increased in value during the marriage or if both spouses worked at it.

• Property purchased with a combination of separate and community funds is part community and part separate property, so long as a spouse is able to trace how separate funds were used. Separate property mixed together with community property generally becomes community property.

What are some of the points that a typical court considers when dividing assets and determining support?
Courts most commonly consider the following issues: the duration of the marriage; the earning power of each party, i.e., how well each of you is equipped to maintain your present standard of living; the marketable skills of the party seeking support; how long the party who has been supported until now has stayed at home; whether children will make it harder for the party seeking support to find work; and what would be involved, i.e., time and expense, to educate or retrain the stay-at-home partner for the current job market. The court's goal is that the party seeking support will eventually be able to support him- or herself. The trend in many states is to award spousal support in longer marriages (i.e., more than seven to ten years), for a period of time equal in length to half the duration of the marriage. The court also considers the means of the partner who is being asked for support, and child-

support and custody arrangements, when applicable. In determining child support, the court often looks to the percentage of time the child or children spend with each parent and the respective incomes of each parent. The court will also consider age, health, and extenuating circumstances, such as whether you're caring for an invalid child or parent. Some courts have schedules that use a percentage of income or an income amount as the basis to set support levels.

My spouse and I have lived in the same house for 12 years. Now that we're getting divorced, how will the court decide who gets to stay and who has to go?

The hardest decision most divorcing couples face is who gets to keep or stay in the home that the two of you lived in together. Who keeps the house and who moves out can be a murky legal area, because the law does not mandate who must move out. Of course, if your name is not on the title, you will have to go.

When there are children involved, it's another story. The primary caretaker usually is allowed to stay in the house with the children until the children reach 18 years of age. If you are the primary caretaker, please see an attorney before you separate from your spouse, because if you have moved out and there's a subsequent legal battle for the house, many judges will lean toward keeping the situation as it is rather than disrupting the children's lives yet again. If there is any physical threat to the children, then you must seek a restraining order that would prevent your spouse from staying in the house. Usually, though, the decision will be made between the two of you, alone or with the aid of legal counsel or a mediator (more about mediators later).

My husband and I have agreed to sell our house rather than haggle over it. How do we figure out how much it is worth?

Many people decide to take this route. Use local resources. Contact a real estate agent and see if he or she can provide some recent sale prices of homes in your neighborhood that are comparable to yours. If you aren't satisfied with the answers you get, you can hire a real estate appraiser. The important thing is not to value your house based on its tax appraisal, because tax appraisals are typically considerably lower than the price your house might actually fetch. If you really have agreed to sell, then the market itself will determine the value. That is, a willing buyer and a willing seller agreeing on a sale price establish the fair market value of a home.

What are the capital-gains rules these days about selling a house?

In 1997, Congress changed the rules regarding capital gains on the sale of your primary residence—in the taxpayer's favor. If you are single, you get a capital-gains exclusion of $250,000. This means you won't be taxed on the first $250,000 of profit from the sale of your house. Married couples may receive an exclusion of $500,000. The only glitch is that you have to have lived in your house for at least two of the five years prior to selling it to be eligible for the exclusion. Keep this time limit in mind if you are thinking of moving out but putting off the sale of the house for a few years. A partial exclusion is available under certain circumstances if you have lived there for less than two years. Consult with your tax adviser. Special rules also apply if you rented the property or used part or all of it for business.

Is this a one-time-only exclusion?

More good news from Congress—no. You can use this exclusion every two years and as many times as you like.

Do I have to "roll over" the proceeds of my sale into a new property?

No. The so-called "rollover" provision, which allowed you to delay paying capital gains only if you agreed to buy a new house of equal or greater value, is almost a thing of the past. If you still have some of the deferred capital gains under the old rules, it can eat up part or all of your exclusion under the new rules.

What happens if my husband and I make more than $500,000 profit from the sale of our house?

As of 2003, thanks to the Jobs and Growth Tax Relief Reconciliation Act of 2003, the amount in excess of the $500,000 exclusion will be taxed at the new capital-gains tax rate, which is 15 percent, or 5 percent for people in the two lowest tax brackets.

How do you divide up the value of your house?

The value of the house is set on the date of divorce, not on the separation date. In other words, let's say you decide that the marriage is over, and you and your spouse separate and you move out. Two years later, the divorce is final. If the value of the house has increased over those two years, you will get to participate in that increase in value.

Can your spouse leave you, move to another state, and sue for divorce there to get a better deal for him- or herself?

Yes. This is why many high-profile figures who divorce try to get the proceedings switched to a community-property state, where the split is fifty-fifty. Bear in mind, though, that laws regarding residency requirements before filing for and being granted a divorce vary widely from state to state.

If I move from one state to another, can my marital property rights change?

Yes, and sometimes drastically. For example, if you move to California and you own marital property in another state, this property may be considered "quasi-community property." Accordingly, you may have to split it equally in the event of a divorce. Quasi-community property is an asset that would be considered community property if it was acquired or located in the state you live in when you divorce, but may not be considered as such in the state where it is located.

In a divorce, can a spouse take back a gift given specifically to you—or at least claim his or her "half" of such a gift?

Not if it really was a gift. But transfers often can be ambiguous, and thus the gift giver may be able to claim that whatever changed hands wasn't really a gift at all.

I suspect my soon-to-be ex-spouse is hiding assets. Is there anything I can do to force him to disclose everything he owns?

In many states there are particular requirements of disclosure for a divorce. If you later discover that there were hidden assets, the court can award all of them to you—not just the 50 percent you might otherwise have expected to be granted. You can always reopen a divorce action if you believe your ex-spouse defrauded you in the settlement. This holds true in every state.

My husband and I were divorced shortly after he declared bankruptcy. Am I protected from his creditors, or can they come after me?

If you live in a community-property state and your husband incurred his debts during your marriage, you are responsible for those debts after divorce—unless the marital settlement agreement states otherwise and the creditor knows of that agreement. Remember, though, there is a statute of limitations on debt, so if his creditors do not sue you within the prescribed time—a period that varies from state to state—they will lose their right to do so. If you do not live in a community-property state and your husband has filed for bankruptcy by himself, you are not liable for his debts.

DIVORCE, RETIREMENT BENEFITS, AND SOCIAL SECURITY

My spouse and I both count our retirement plans among our assets. At what point does the court begin to assess the value of our retirement plans?

Many states value retirement plans and/or benefits from the date of separation, not from the date of divorce, because this date marks the point at which a couple's common interest and mutual support ended. Keep this in mind because it may affect what you and your spouse are entitled to. For instance, many employers make their contributions to their employees' pension plans at the end of the calendar year. If you separated from your spouse and moved out on December 24, and on December 25 your spouse's employer made the annual retirement plan contribution, you might very well have missed out on your right to claim any portion of that year's contribution. (Many self-employed people put the year's retirement money into their Keoghs or SEP-IRAs at the very last minute of the tax year, so also take that into consideration.)

Make sure, then, that you know how your and/or your spouse's retirement plan works. When are the valuations of it made? Where a retirement plan is involved, consult an attorney before making any move and obtain a copy of the benefit schedule for both your and your spouse's retirement plan.

My husband and I are divorced, and I don't have a substantial work record of my own. Is it possible for me to claim Social Security based on his record?

You are eligible to receive dependents benefits if you and your ex-spouse are 62 years of age or older, your marriage lasted for at least ten years, and the marriage was dissolved at least two years before you make a claim (this refers to the actual date that your divorce became final). Please note, however, that this two-year waiting period does not apply if your ex-spouse was already receiving retirement benefits prior to your divorce. When your ex-spouse becomes eligible for retirement benefits at age 62, you can begin collecting dependents benefits.

Timing is everything here. Again, let me share a recent memory. A woman I know decided that she wanted to divorce her husband, and she wanted to do it immediately. Luckily, the divorce promised to be very amicable. They had seen an attorney and had papers drawn up, which she was about to sign when she called to ask me a question about their investments. I asked her how long they had been married, and she told me nearly ten years. I suggested she wait, because if she went ahead and signed those papers right away, she would not, when the time came, be entitled to Social Security benefits based on her spouse's earnings. Social Security benefits are based on the date of divorce, not the date of separation. Since my client had never worked outside the home and hadn't built up Social Security of her own, signing the divorce papers before their tenth anniversary would have turned out to be a big mistake. If she wanted to, I told her, she could move out, they could separate, and for all intents and purposes they could go on with their lives as if they were divorced. Then, after their tenth anniversary, they could sign all the necessary papers to make the divorce legal.

Waiting to pass the ten-year mark affected not only my client's Social Security but also her alimony. The seven-to-ten-year mark is important because many states use these anniversaries as benchmarks for what constitutes a long-term marriage. In the case of a spouse who has not worked outside the home or who was earning very little during the marriage, a long-term marriage judgment may be very favorable for purposes of spousal support.

What if my former spouse decides to wait until age 65 to claim his Social Security benefits? Does this mean that I have to wait, too?

No. Your former spouse must merely become *eligible* for his or her retirement benefits for you to begin collecting dependents benefits.

What percentage of my ex-husband's Social Security benefits will I get?

If there is no other previous ex-wife receiving dependents benefits and if your ex-husband was born before 1937, then you will receive approximately 50 percent of your ex-husband's retirement or disability benefits. If he was born later, you will receive between 20 percent and 30 percent of those benefits. To make absolutely certain what benefits you will be receiving, you should order a Social Security statement.

*Does the amount that I get in Social Security depend-
ents benefits have any effect on the amount that my
former spouse will be receiving in retirement benefits?*

No. It is important to understand that by claiming these benefits, you are not in any way "punishing" your former spouse.
Your dependents benefits will not take away from any of the
money he or she will collect. You are simply getting what you
are entitled to by law.

*What if I remarry and lose my Social Security depend-
ents benefits, but my second marriage doesn't last? Can
I reclaim those original dependents benefits?*

Yes. And if your second marriage lasted for more than ten
years, too, then you could very possibly be eligible to claim
dependents benefits based on your second husband's work
record. You can choose the benefits of either husband as long
as you did not marry a third time before the age of 60.

*If my former spouse dies, will my Social Security
dependents benefits continue?*

Yes, though they will automatically become survivors benefits.

*If my former spouse remarries, will this have any
effect on my Social Security dependents benefits?*

No.

*What criteria do I have to meet in order to be eligible
for my former husband's Social Security benefits?*

Curiously enough, this is a matter that you have to work out
with the Social Security Administration, not with your former
spouse. You may very well be entitled to retirement benefits if
you are at least 62 years old, are not married when you apply
for benefits, are not already receiving Social Security spousal or
survivors benefits, and were married for at least ten years.

How do I establish my eligibility for Social Security benefits?

You should visit the Social Security office nearest where you live at least three months before you turn 62. You should bring along with you proof of your identity, your age (as well as the age of your former spouse), your marriage, and your divorce. You can also apply online at https://s044a90.ssa.gov/apps6z/ISBA/main.html.

COLLABORATIVE LAW

I have heard the term "collaborative law." What does it mean?

Collaborative law is a fairly new option for working out all the issues involved in your divorce. It involves you, your spouse, and your attorneys sitting down together to hammer out a divorce settlement that is fair to you and your spouse. (The attorneys must have training in the collaborative law process.) Collaborative law is now available in all but a few states— Montana, Wyoming, and South Dakota—and it is catching on rapidly worldwide.

What are the benefits of collaborative law?

For one thing, it can be cheaper and less anxiety-provoking than using either a mediator or an arbitrator. It's also an amicable way for you and your spouse to settle your differences, and it can pave the way toward a much more cooperative relationship in the future, which is particularly important when there are children involved.

What are the disadvantages of collaborative law?

One of the biggest drawbacks of collaborative law is that if it doesn't work and you end up needing the court to step in and intervene, both your attorney and your husband's attorney must agree to recuse themselves from your case. Basically, you'll each have to hire a new attorney and start all over again. Another risk is that the dynamics of your relationship with your ex— for example, his tendency to bully you—may be replicated in the collaborative-law situation.

What is the difference between this method and using a mediator?
The difference is that a mediator is a neutral third party, whereas in collaborative law, there is no neutral third party present.

MEDIATION

My attorney has suggested that my husband and I explore the possibility of using a mediator. Do you advise this?
I usually recommend trying mediation for at least one session. A mediator can help you decide how your property is going to be divided and can also be very helpful in resolving custody arrangements. A mediator is a kind of counselor or referee and, just like a ref, he or she is impartial, with no allegiance to either you or your husband, and works to help you both reach a fair, consensual resolution. Please realize that if you are able to reach an agreement with the help of a mediator, it will probably be necessary for you to have your attorneys finalize the agreement and submit it to the court to ensure that it will be legally binding.

Are mediators lawyers?
Many mediators are attorneys, but others come from a variety of backgrounds. They can be psychologists, social workers,

marriage counselors, clergymen, or financial experts. They do not need to be licensed, but in some states they do need to have received specialized training in mediation. To locate a mediator in your state, contact the Association for Conflict Resolution at *acrnet.org*.

In what circumstances would a mediator not be helpful?

I would not recommend a mediator in cases where custody arrangements or the division of property are unusually complicated, or in cases where emotions are running so high that you and your spouse can't work together. If you are afraid of your spouse for any reason, I would stay away from mediation. I would also keep away from a mediator if you do not feel sure of what your priorities and goals are with respect to negotiation. You should use a mediator only if you and your spouse are able to engage in rational discussion and if you believe you can reach a general agreement about how you want to split things up.

How much do mediators charge?

Depending on what part of the country you live in and the experience and reputation of the mediator in question, he or she will charge anywhere from $60 to $300 an hour. Mediation can work in as few as two hours, or it can last several months, with several sessions scheduled each week.

What happens if mediation works out?

If things work out, then your mediator will usually formalize your agreement in writing. He or she will give each of your attorneys a copy of the agreement to review, and if they give their go-ahead, both of you will sign it. The mediation agreement will be incorporated into your divorce agreement. In some instances, the agreement is signed right after the mediation is concluded, especially if your attorneys have been present during the negotiations.

ARBITRATION

What is the difference between a mediator and an arbitrator? In what situation would it be wise to use an arbitrator?

If you are in a situation where you don't want your divorce to go to trial in a formal courtroom but are concerned that your spouse may manage to get the mediator to see things his way, you might want to seek out an arbitrator. An arbitrator is frequently an attorney, but can also be a retired judge or therapist. Like mediation, arbitration is a private matter. Only the fact of a resolution becomes part of the public record. In both mediation and arbitration, you avoid going to court, but that's where the similarity ends. Mediation is usually a conciliatory process: You and your spouse agree on who gets what, and in the end, despite the unavoidable pain of divorce, you both leave satisfied. Most important, the mediator has no power to grant a decision. Arbitration is different because, by definition, the arbitrator can impose a decision on the division of property, just as a judge does. The only differences between an arbitrator and a judge are that you and your spouse select the arbitrator and pay his or her fees rather than using a government-appointed judge, and usually you cannot appeal an arbitrator's decision. To locate an arbitrator in your area, you can get in touch with the American Arbitration Association at *www.adr.org*.

That doesn't sound so bad. What are the drawbacks of hiring an arbitrator?

Mediation is typically much faster than arbitration, in large part because both parties have agreed to conduct themselves in an amicable way. In effect, you and your spouse are in charge of the outcome. Arbitration, like a court trial, takes that power out of your hands. Remember, the arbitrator is legally allowed to make far-reaching decisions about the allocation of your assets, based on evidence, the facts presented to him or her, and the laws in your particular state. With arbitration, the process is less formal than it would be in court, and usually you pay less in attorneys' fees, but you each have to pay half the arbitrator's fee. Also, you will have to live with whatever decisions the arbitrator makes. Finally, some people fear that since arbitrators are not really judges, they aren't as qualified to render fair decisions.

Are mediation and arbitration the only two options for us unless my husband and I agree to go to court?

Well, there's also a "marriage" of mediation and arbitration techniques. It's called "med/arb," and it's a little of both. The "med" part assumes that you and your husband will try to work things out in as amicable a way as possible. If this fails, the mediator becomes an "arb," and can make decisions on your and your husband's behalf.

THE REALITIES OF DIVORCE

Both my husband and I want to get our divorce over with as quickly and painlessly as possible. What happens after we've met with our attorneys and discussed all our assets and liabilities?

Once you've met with your attorneys and discussed your assets and liabilities, it's time to negotiate the settlement. If the marriage has been very short, no real property is involved, there are no children, and there aren't a lot of assets (or debts) to divide, you may be able to divorce through a summary disposition, which is basically the quickest, most efficient way to file for divorce. In a summary disposition, you and your spouse agree on the basic terms of the dissolution and jointly file simple paperwork with the local court, setting forth your plans. Usually, the actual filing is done without an attorney (self-representation in legal terms is known as "in pro per"), though in some cases even a summary disposition is done with attorneys or with a joint attorney overseeing the paperwork. In most states, the judge or a research assistant will review the documents and attempt to verify that the agreement is a fair one. (Remember, you can't get a summary dissolution if there are children involved!) In some states you may not even have to show up for a court hearing; in other states a brief hearing may be held, so that the judge can ensure that both sides are getting a fair deal.

What about those cases when a divorce is not friendly?
In these cases, it is not just a good idea for each of you to have an attorney—it is a must. In some cases, even attorneys will not be able to hammer out an agreement, and the two of you will have to go before a judge. The attorney's role, as always, is to represent your interests, suggest appropriate settlement terms, convey settlement offers, advise you as to what the court is likely to do in your situation, and help with the division of property and debts. The attorney does everything he or she would do in an amicable situation and also fights your battles for you and insulates you from your estranged spouse. Once the terms have been decided—who gets what and when—either by the two of you or with a court order, a marital settlement agreement,

stipulated judgment, or court's final judgment of divorce is drafted, signed by the parties and lawyers, and finally signed by a judge, which makes it a legally binding order. If you cannot come to an agreement, you will end up settling your dispute in court.

It looks like my spouse and I are headed toward court. What should I keep in mind?
You should know that when it comes to divorce, the court system is set up to make sure that the division of property is handled fairly and to ensure the welfare of any children involved. When you go to court, the outcome is solely in the hands of the judge. This means that you are putting the fate of your future, your home, your children, and your pension and retirement plans in the hands of a total stranger. You should also know that the court usually doesn't care whose "fault" the divorce is!

Are you saying that my husband and I should really try our best to work out the terms of our divorce instead of going to court?
Yes. It won't be easy—in fact, it will be emotional and probably very difficult—but, in my opinion, if you and your spouse can agree on terms between yourselves and reach a clear resolution, you may very well be better off than you would be entrusting your fate and your future to an unknown judge. But if you simply cannot resolve your differences, you shouldn't be afraid to put the matter in the hands of a court.

If my wife and I are already in court, heading toward trial, is there any way to reach a settlement of some kind at this point, or is there no turning back?
There is always room to "turn back" and reach a settlement.

Turning back isn't a failure; it's a solution—and, in a lot of cases, a wise one. Even if you are committed to taking your spouse to court, an out-of-court settlement may be reached days or perhaps minutes before the case is to begin. In fact, 90 percent of divorces are settled before trial, no matter how hell-bent both parties are on having a judge hear their case. However, I ask you to be very careful, because this is the time when big mistakes are often made. Imagine this scenario: You are about to go into the courtroom, nervous as can be. Your lawyer, who has been talking in hushed tones with the lawyer representing your ex, approaches you and says your ex is willing to settle the case right now if you give in on a few points. The decision has to be made right away, because once the trial begins it is too late. So you give in on the points and instantly feel a wave of relief. Two months down the road, however, you realize that you may have made a mistake solely to avoid a courtroom confrontation. Do not make decisions that will affect the rest of your life when you feel pressured. If you have gone all the way to trial, do not—unless you know the precise ramifications of everything you are agreeing to—accept a last-minute settlement.

With our court date just a few weeks away, my estranged husband has offered me a certain amount of money in a onetime payoff. This seems to be more attractive than receiving money from him every month because I can put him and our marriage behind me. Any advice?

In some instances, a spouse may offer a onetime, lump-sum offer of settlement, which in effect is a "buyout" of any future obligations, excluding child support. A once-and-for-all settlement needs to be looked at with caution, because the spouse required to pay is using today's dollars to settle what might be a significantly greater amount tomorrow. If you are considering a settlement, consider all the factors and make sure you get professional advice. You also need to check out all the tax implications of such an arrangement.

Six months after I filed for divorce, my day in court is finally here. I am extremely nervous. What happens during a trial?

Courtroom trials are fairly predictable and never particularly fluid—that is, they stop and start and stop again. After opening statements, the court hears the case of the plaintiff (that's you, the person who filed for divorce). This is followed by a cross-examination by the attorney for the defendant (your spouse), which is followed by redirect (your attorney's chance to cross-examine the cross-examination). Next, the defendant's case is presented, followed by a rebuttal by the plaintiff's attorney, and then, typically, there are closing arguments. Depending on how complex your case is, the judge may issue his or her decision immediately or choose to deliberate for a while and then issue a written decision.

What happens after the judge issues his or her decision?

Usually the attorney for the person who prevailed in court drafts a divorce decree. A divorce decree is basically a summary of the judge's decision, which also includes whatever matters you and your spouse decided between yourselves. After the decree is sent to the opposing counsel for approval, it is submitted to the court for its approval.

Can my ex-husband or I appeal the judge's decision?

If you have a legal basis for appeal, of course you can. You cannot mount an appeal simply because you don't happen to like his or her decision. Remember, an appeal takes time and money, and the trial court's decision is rarely overturned. For people who have just spent a lot of money on attorneys' fees, the notion of spending even more money—and prolonging the agony of divorce—often doesn't seem very appealing. A much more efficient way to deal with the aspects of the judge's decision regarding alimony or child custody and support issues that rub you the wrong way is to file a petition for modification based on changed circumstances. This basically leaves the judge's decision in place, but requests that the court modify one or more provisions that you do not like. Also, in some states, within a short period of time after the court judgment, a motion for reconsideration based on new evidence may be made.

Does the divorce decree affect any pretrial court orders?

Yes. Typically, it replaces them.

Assuming that neither of us appeals the judge's decision, now what?

Now a record of your divorce decree is filed at the county courthouse and you are officially divorced. For better or for worse. This is the time to make sure that all your documents—the deed to your house, the title to your car or boat, your will or trust, your insurance policies, retirement plans, IRAs, and every investment or asset that was previously held jointly—reflect your new status. Please don't let this paperwork slide, for decisiveness will help the healing and make you feel stronger for having put your past behind you. With the clutter gone, you'll be freer to put your energies into starting over again.

LIFE AFTER SEPARATION
AND DIVORCE

For years my husband and I filed joint tax returns.
Now that we're no longer separated, do I simply go
back to filing singly? If so, at what point do I start
doing this?

Any and all income you earn from the date of separation may,
if you choose, be filed on a separate tax return. There may be
tax ramifications, possibly negative, when you decide to do
this, so make sure you consult an accountant. If you still have
any doubt as to what you should do, or if you and your spouse
cannot decide how you should file your taxes, file separately.
The law allows people who file separately to amend their taxes
within a three-year period and to file again jointly, but the law
does not let people who file jointly amend their taxes later to
file separately. You can't file a joint return in the year your
divorce decree or legal separation agreement is final.

If you file taxes separately, you and your spouse must decide
together how you will divide deductions—the home mortgage
interest, charitable deductions that you made together, property taxes, day-care expenses, etc. You will also need to allocate
income from joint accounts to one or both spouses for next
year's tax returns.

When filing jointly, each of you is liable for what the other
puts on your tax return. Be particularly wary if you distrust
your spouse when it comes to money. If your spouse overstates
deductions or understates income and the IRS catches it, you
as well as your spouse may be held responsible for all back
taxes and penalties, plus interest. If your now ex-spouse cannot

pay these back taxes and penalties, the IRS may, with certain exceptions, come after you. So if money has been a problem between the two of you, you might want to protect yourself and file separately for peace of mind, even if it will cost you more.

My ex-wife is getting in the way of my visitation rights with my children. What should I do?

I will tell you what you should not do, and that is withhold money that the court ordered you to send her for child support. That is not only breaking the law, it could also threaten your children's well-being. If you and your ex-wife aren't speaking to each other and can't work this out in a civil way, then you must bring a contempt-of-court action against her. Unless your ex can prove that she has very good reasons for keeping you away from your kids, she will be ordered by the court to do what is legal and may have to pay your legal costs and a fine, and possibly face going to jail in a short period.

My husband is continually late with his child-support payments. Is there anything I can do?

Unfortunately, you are not alone. The legal term for past-due child support is arrearage, and it is a national shame. If I were you, I would hire an attorney to go after your husband, assuming he has some money to chase after. A less expensive method is to contact your state's Child Support Enforcement (CSE) program. The federal website, *www.acf.dhhs.gov,* has links to state agencies.

If your spouse is behind in child-support payments, you may be able to engage the help of a government official, either someone from the IRS or a child-support-enforcement advocate, to seize the assets of your errant spouse. Whether to hire your own attorney or rely on the government depends on the laws of your particular state.

What about these private child-support collection agencies I keep reading about in the newspaper?
Working with one of these agencies is a possibility, but I would check out the fees very carefully first. Some take a huge chunk of any money they recover on behalf of your children.

THE DEATH OF A LOVED ONE

For those of you who are in a position to learn about your finances from your loved ones, I beg you not to put this topic off one minute longer. Discuss with your spouse or partner everything you need to know about your estate—including insurance, the children's best interests, the location of all documents, and a list of whom to notify—before one of you dies. I urge you both to make your preferences clear—whether you wish to be buried or cremated, where you would like your remains to rest, and what kind of service or ceremony you would like to have. A loved one's death is overwhelming, but having some of the details worked out and a sense of purpose in those first painful days will provide some relief to whichever one of you survives.

When you have just suffered a loss, it's not the time to start learning about money. When you are in a marriage or other close relationship, it is vital—and I cannot stress this enough—that both of you know everything there is to know about your money. Not only how to spend it, but how to invest it and why. Both of you should know where all your important documents are and should know the answer to this question: If one of you were to die tomorrow, would there be enough income for the other person to be financially secure? Please ask this question while your partner is still around to answer it.

Little by little, step by step, you can and must learn to handle your money and make decisions that will be right for you in the long run.

My husband of six years recently died after a short, unexpected illness. I feel utterly wiped out emotionally. How can I start to put my life in order?

To have someone you love taken from you forever creates a pain so deep that there is often little anyone can say or do to help. Having faced the emotional and financial aftermath of death many times with former clients, I have come to believe that we never quite know the meaning of life until we draw close to death. Everything is put into perspective and yet, in our grief, most of us put thoughts of money out of our minds, which can be a terrible mistake. The death of a partner forces us not only to deal with a new emotional reality, but also to accept a new financial reality.

I am totally unprepared to deal with financial matters in the midst of all this emotion! Do you have any suggestions?

Allow yourself time to grieve and to heal—but be mindful that the longer you neglect the financial consequences of a spouse's death, the harder it will be to pick up the pieces once you feel ready to take charge. Over the years, I have been called upon many times to reassemble a client's financial life after a spouse's death. Some people who came to me were lucky; when their spouses or life partners died, they had a friend or someone they could trust to help them along on their new financial course. But many bereaved men and women had sought the advice of a so-called professional when they were most vulnerable and ended up losing everything, or nearly so. By the time they found their way to me, these people had handed over their life insurance proceeds, their portfolios—their futures—to con artists posing as concerned advisers or to commission-hungry salespeople. It is hard enough to find the courage to go on after you have lost your emotional equilibrium, but it is almost impossible when you have lost your financial stability, too. Difficult as it may seem to you now, in the early stages of your grief, I ask you please to keep your financial realities in mind as you come to terms with the death of your spouse or life partner. The actions you take at this time will have important effects later, when the death and your grief are not so new and raw.

My mother, who is 70, lives in Florida and has a burial plot in New York. She recently called and asked me if I thought it was wise for her to prepay her funeral expenses. She has been quoted a package that would send her body back to New York and pay for the chapel, the rabbi, and the cemetery fees, all for less than $4,000. What should I tell her?

Well, my first words of advice would be for you to look at some basic numbers. Actuarially speaking, your mother is likely to live another 17 years. If she takes that $4,000 today and invests it in a good no-load mutual fund that averages a 10 percent return, in 17 years that $4,000 will be worth $20,218. If you adjust for inflation at, say, 3 percent, that $20,218 would still be worth $12,232 in today's dollars. And not only does she lose the investment potential of her $4,000, but buying this package leaves her no room to change her mind about her funeral arrangements. What if she meets a wonderful man in Florida, marries him, and decides she would like to be buried with him? The short answer to your question is, I think prepaid funerals are a waste of money.

My wife just died very suddenly, and my children and I are devastated. It's hard to think about funeral arrangements at this time, but I have no choice. Where should I start?

Losing someone you love can be paralyzing—but you must take care of the business of death, which can seem as complicated as the business of life. Here is a checklist of matters that will require your immediate attention, whether you feel like attending to them or not. If you have a friend or a relative who can assist you, please ask for help. Even though you may think you are capable and thinking clearly, you are probably in shock.

- The first job that you will be faced with will be making proper arrangements for the burial or cremation of the person you loved. (If you are not certain of the deceased's wishes, before you do anything else, please check to see if there is an organ donor designation on his or her driver's license. If there is, please contact the nearest hospital so that these wishes can be carried out.) You must contend with the remains, surely one of the most painful tasks you'll have to perform, but I want you to take care and pay attention, for these first moves can become emotionally and financially costly if you or someone close to you is not vigilant and well informed.
- If the death took place in a hospital, you will be asked the name of the funeral home that you would like to use. The hospital staff will call the funeral home and take care of transporting the remains to the home.
- If the death took place at your home or anywhere other than a hospital, you will have to contact the funeral home or cremation society of your choice, which will then make arrangements to transport the remains.

- If you want the burial or cremation to take place in a state different from the one in which your loved one has died, again, either you or the hospital will place the call to the out-of-state funeral home or cremation society you want to use, and they will take care of the transportation arrangements for you.
- If you don't know which funeral home you want to use, ask your friends, your clergyman, or an administrator at your local place of worship for a recommendation. Most churches or synagogues have a list of funeral homes for you to call. If you do not have this resource and none of your friends can make a recommendation, call your local hospital for assistance.

I've heard horror stories about funeral homes ripping off grieving survivors. When I go in, what should I be aware of?

Many years ago the government passed a law called the Funeral Rule, which states that a funeral home must provide you with a full disclosure of its practices, services, and fees. This includes the cost of caskets, obituary notices placed in newspapers, and embalming; any payments made on your behalf for flowers, funeral escorts, honorarium to clergy, limousines, copies of the death certificate, memorial cards, and musicians' fees; and any additional service fee that the funeral home may charge. If you wish, you can obtain this list from a number of funeral homes so that you can compare costs. If you choose a funeral home and are not happy with the available funeral arrangements, please talk to the funeral director first, and if the problem is not resolved to your satisfaction, contact your state licensing board.

The service can be held at the funeral home or in a place of worship. If you know what kind of service your partner wanted, so much the better. One often hears of people who choose the music they'd like to have played at their funeral services, and the survivors cherish that music forever. The burial can be public or private, and you can hold a private burial right away and a memorial service later on.

Unless you or someone else planned for the final disposition of the remains ahead of time, the funeral home or cremation society will discuss with you whether you need a burial plot and also can assist you in making arrangements to purchase one.

How much should I spend on a funeral?

That's up to you, of course, but when it comes to planning the service, carefully consider your options. You shouldn't try to prove your love by choosing the most expensive options available; in fact, you should take into consideration your available resources and immediate future expenses before you make any choices regarding funeral or burial services. For instance, let's say you have $8,000 in a savings account and your expenses for the next month will total $3,000. If you spend $8,000 on the funeral, you'll be unable to pay your bills. Dignity, remember, costs not a penny. Public and private good-byes can be dignified, holy, and simple at the same time.

My husband is a veteran of two wars, and I'd like to know beforehand how I can arrange a proper veteran's burial when the time comes.

If your partner or loved one was a veteran, he or she may be eligible to be buried in any of the 115 national cemeteries, free of charge. If so, veterans' assistance may provide transportation of the remains to the nearest veterans' cemetery and a marker or a headstone. In a veteran's burial, a U.S. flag will be used to cover the casket and then will be presented to you. If you choose a veteran's burial, you will have to document the fact that the deceased was a veteran. You will need to have proof of his or her:

Rank
Branch of service
Separation papers (Form DD-214)
Date of entry into the service and date of departure
Date of birth and date of death
Social Security number (as well as your own)
Name and address of the executor or trustee of the estate

Can I choose to have my husband buried in a private cemetery as opposed to a national one and still have a military funeral?
Yes. If you use a private cemetery, you still can apply for a burial allowance, a flag, and a government headstone or marker from the Department of Veterans Affairs. If you did not know of such an allowance at the time of burial, you have two years from the date of death to apply for a reimbursement. To apply, just look in your phone book to find the number of the VA office nearest you. For more information, log on to *www.cem.va.gov*.

My husband was buried only last month. Now comes the hard part—settling back into my life. Any ideas on where to start?
When you are trying to live through a loss of great magnitude, it is all too easy to lose touch with practical matters—especially those touching on money. Yet money continues to be important. After the funeral and during your period of mourning, how are you going to pay for the everyday expenses? Often people find that nearly every penny they have is in a retirement

account, in a life insurance policy, or locked up in equity in a home, where they can't readily get to it. They can be left with very little cash to draw from. If you haven't done so before, you will now have to try to estimate your monthly expenses and be sure that you can pay them while matters concerning your husband's estate are settled.

My husband left me a life insurance policy. Won't this take care of things for the short term?

Even if the deceased had a life insurance policy, the insurance company might not release the funds for many months. This is particularly the case if the cause of death is unclear or if the death appears to have been a suicide. I have a friend whose brother died in a car-racing accident. It just so happened that he had raised his life insurance policy from $50,000 to $250,000 the month before his accident. Because of the timing, the insurance company did not release the insurance proceeds until it had thoroughly investigated the possibility of a suicide. In the intervening months, his widow was left in terrible financial straits.

So I should be very careful before I start spending what I think I have?

Yes. Before you do anything, it is essential that you have a clear picture of what you are going to need to get by for the next few months and where that money is going to come from. My advice, as always, is to have an understanding of your finances long before you find yourself in a tragic situation.

All my friends are offering to pitch in and help me. Should I take them up on their offers?

Most definitely. That's what friends are for. Following a death, I would suggest you ask whomever you have chosen to help you with the funeral arrangements to collect your mail for the next few weeks. It would also be helpful if he or she could see if there are any bills that need to be paid immediately and keep track of when the rest of the bills will come due. If you are corresponding through the mail about financial matters related to the estate, please ask your friend to make sure that copies are made of letters and documents being sent by you. It is always important to be able to document anything that you have said or that has been said on your behalf during a time of sorrow. Later you may remember these early days only as a blur of pain and confusion.

Do I need to contact an attorney, or can I do everything myself?

The way your spouse has set up his or her estate will determine the extent to which you will need the help of an attorney. If everything the two of you owned was in joint tenancy with right of survivorship (JTWROS) and you are the sole beneficiary of the life insurance proceeds, IRA, or retirement accounts, everything will automatically pass directly to you upon your spouse's death. Similarly, if all your joint assets were held for your benefit in a revocable living trust (a legal entity that holds your assets while you are alive), then settling the estate will be easy. (For more information on JTWROS, please see *Ask Suze . . . About Wills and Trusts.*) Once the appropriate institutions are presented with a certified copy of the death certificate and whatever other papers they may want to see, everything will simply and automatically be switched over to your name. However, there may be decisions to be made about taxes that will require the immediate assistance of an attorney.

My husband had lots of different accounts. He didn't have a living trust. Will settling his estate take longer?

Unfortunately, yes. If your partner kept a variety of separate accounts, had only a will, and held the house title in his or her name only (even if the intent was that it should pass on to you), then the process will be a longer one. You should contact an attorney within the first few days after your spouse's death. If you do not have an attorney, please find one who specializes in probate administration to make sure that everything is in order and to help you organize what must be done.

So I will need an attorney. Is there anything I can do to save time and money?

Yes—particularly to save money. There are certain tasks that you can complete on your own or with the help of a friend. For example, a friend could call the insurance companies and the bank or brokerage firms to find out what paperwork needs to be completed to report the death. The most important part of your immediate job will be helping to locate and describe all of your loved one's assets and liabilities—debts, outstanding loans, everything your loved one owned and owed to the world.

Now that my husband has died, I'm hearing many new words whose meanings I'm not sure of. Could you translate a few of them for me?

The legalese of death can sometimes seem like a foreign language. Below are brief definitions of some of the terms you will probably come across.

Decedent: The person who is deceased.

Executor/Executrix: The man or woman the decedent designated to carry out the terms of the will.

Co-executors/Co-executrixes: The people (sometimes more than one) the decedent designated to carry out the terms of the will.

Administrator/Administratrix: The person the court assigns to oversee your estate or your spouse's estate if there is no will.

Personal Representative: In some states this is the title of the court appointee, whether a man or a woman.

Trustee: When the estate is held in trust, this is the person who is responsible for carrying out the terms of the trust.

What precisely are my duties and responsibilities as the survivor, both to my late spouse and to myself?

The duties that a spouse or life partner must carry out vary from those of the executor or executrix. Here is an overview of what you, the survivor, should be attending to immediately:

- Order at least 15 certified copies of the death certificate. You will need these in order to collect insurance proceeds and to change names on bank accounts, deeds, and other assets. Please do this right away. The funeral home usually will be able to obtain the number of certified death certificates you request. Otherwise, your county has an office of vital statistics at the county courthouse, where death, birth, and marriage certificates are kept and can be obtained upon request for a fee.

- If you do not already have one, please open a bank account in your own name.

- If you do not have a credit card in your own name, you may want to wait to notify the credit card companies where you have cards listed in both of your names. While it is illegal for a company to cancel your credit card because your spouse has died, it is not unheard of for a company to lower your credit limit if the limit was based on the deceased's income. (It's always a good idea to have a credit card in your name alone so that, over the years, you will build up a credit history.)

- Do not pay off any credit card debts that were not yours alone before you check with your attorney or executor. Some attorneys or advisers might counsel you not to pay off the deceased's debts because it's unlikely that creditors will spend the money to come after the estate to recoup small amounts of debt. I disagree with this advice because I believe that honoring a debt, when possible, is honoring both the dead and the living. If there isn't enough money in the estate to pay off all debts, the probate court has a "schedule" specifying which debts are given priority and the order in which the debts are to be paid—which is why I want you to check with your attorney before you begin paying any debts.

- Review any insurance coverage that the deceased may have had with banks or credit card companies. You may have more than you know. For instance, offers for life insurance at just a small cost every month often come in the mail via a bank statement or credit card bill. Your spouse may have impulsively signed up for such coverage. This kind of thing happens more often than you might think. Call every credit card company and bank that the deceased had accounts with and ask whether they also have an insurance policy in the name of the deceased.

- Consider whether you will have enough money to live on in the coming months or will need money from the estate before it is settled. Go through six months of your and your late spouse's records and estimate your monthly expenses. If there is not enough money in your existing accounts to cover your projected expenses, the amount you need will be requested from a judge in probate court. The judge will decide on a family allowance while the estate is being settled.

- Contact your local Social Security office—or call the national office at (800) 772-1213 or log on to the Web at *www.ssa.gov*—to see if you qualify for any benefits. You will qualify for benefits if:

You are 60 years of age or older.
You are 50 years of age or older and disabled.
You care for a child who is under age 16 or disabled.

If your surviving parent is 62 years of age or older, and you are your parent's primary means of support, you will qualify through Social Security for survivor's benefits.

In addition, Social Security allots a small amount of money—$255—to surviving spouses or minors if they meet certain requirements. Do not overlook that, for sometimes every little bit can help.

If you and your spouse both were collecting Social Security, you might want to stop collecting yours and collect your late spouse's if that amount is higher. In any case, you have to choose whose you will receive.

Your children will get Social Security if:
They are unmarried and under age 18.
They are under age 19 and still in school full-time.
They are disabled, no matter how old they are.

- Please make a note: Do not forget that your own will or trust should be changed now, for most likely you have left everything to the person who has just died. Make sure that you change the beneficiary designation on your IRA, life insurance policies, pension plans, 401(k) plans, and any other investment or retirement plans.

I am both the surviving spouse of my late husband and also one of the executors of his estate. Do I have duties in addition to the ones you just named above?

If you are an executor or executrix as well as the surviving spouse, then the following obligations also pertain. Please note that an executor is held personally and legally responsible for all of the actions associated with these duties. This is not a job that should be taken lightly or treated as honorary. The duties of the executor primarily fall into the following categories:

- Paying all outstanding bills, including taxes to the IRS.
- Tallying and securing all assets in the estate until they are ready to be distributed among the rightful heirs.
- Supervising the settlement procedures and managing the estate during this process.
- Distributing all the assets to the designated beneficiaries at the appropriate time.

The following is a legal checklist for the executor.

- Your first job as executor is to locate the will or trust and all assets, including life insurance policies, retirement, bank, and brokerage accounts, and stocks and bonds. If no will or trust can be found, then call the deceased's attorney, if there is one, to see if he or she has a copy of a will or trust. If nothing else, an attorney may know if one was ever written. (Please note: If no will can be found, the estate passes by what is known as intestate succession, which means that the assets in the estate that would otherwise be subject to a will will be distributed by a formula determined by law. In this case, there will be a court-appointed administrator.)

- If the will is located, it must be submitted to the probate court, where it must be validated by a judge. When the will is proved and admitted to probate, then the executor is officially appointed by a document known as letters testamentary. This is the official document that legally empowers the executor to take action on behalf of the estate.

- The executor must protect the estate. This means that heirs are not allowed to remove any of the assets that have been left to them until the probate court grants final approval for distribution, unless an earlier distribution is allowed by the judge or by law.

- During the probate procedure, the executor must keep careful track of all expenses as well as income (receipts, statements, etc.) that the estate pays out and receives.

- If the surviving spouse has not already obtained certified copies of the death certificate, you should obtain at least 15 copies.

- Notify all the insurance companies of the death, including life, disability, auto, and homeowner's insurance companies. Notify all the banks, brokerage firms, mutual fund companies, retirement plans and plan administrators, and any other institution where the decedent had accounts or deeds, or even accounts that were in both spouses' names. This includes the Department of Veterans Affairs, if the decedent was a veteran.

- Often individual bank accounts in the decedent's name will be changed first to the name of the executor, even if the executor is not the spouse, so that the executor can access funds if needed. However, if a joint tenancy with right of survivorship is involved, the money and title of the account will go directly to the surviving spouse or partner. For example, Jane and John have a bank account held in JTWROS. If John were to die, Jane would get the account immediately. However, if John had an account in his name alone, and John's brother were executor of John's will, the account would first be transferred to his brother's name as executor while the estate was being settled, even if John left everything to Jane. The account would be transferred to Jane's name upon settlement, as the sole beneficiary.

- Before any accounts are closed, please make sure that the financial needs of the surviving spouse are going to be met. It is best to clear it with the attorney before closing existing accounts.
- Make a complete inventory of the decedent's safe-deposit box. As part of the probate process, the executor will distribute the contents according to the will. If the key cannot be located and the surviving spouse's name is not on the box, you won't be able to open it without a court order, although some states permit access to look for such estate-planning documents as wills and trusts. Most states don't seal the boxes anymore, but the bank can make access difficult. If the box is held in the trust, the trustee will have access. Without the key, you will always end up paying the bank $150 or more to "drill" the box open. (Please don't make those you leave behind go through this. Leave the key and instructions with your other easy-to-find documents for your family members or whoever is going to be the executor or trustee of your estate.)

Remember, if the estate is to be distributed through a living trust and the deceased's assets were transferred to the trust during his or her lifetime, it does not have to go through probate court, and the trustee named in the trust will carry out the actions designated in the trust.

STARTING OVER
AFTER A DIVORCE OR THE
DEATH OF A LOVED ONE

My husband died several months ago. What should I be keeping in mind during this period?

Take good care of yourself. Starting over from a place of loss can be even harder than starting out for the first time. When you were first entering your adult life, you were equipped with hope, ideals, expectations, and strength. These are undependable commodities when you're starting over with feelings of loss and emptiness. Will any of us be spared the painful test of starting over, one way or another, one day or another? I don't think so. This test seems universal to me.

As a financial planner, I do know this much: If you are starting over, you already know that you must replenish your strength. It is a treacherous time, financially as well as emotionally, and you must be very, very careful with your money. Facing the "whats" and "what-ifs" of starting over requires immense courage. Questions such as these come up:

- What if I can't make it? I've never really handled money before.
- I've never had to work. What if I can't pay my bills?
- My husband left me with just a small settlement, and it's all I have.

- What should I do with the money?
- What if the insurance money doesn't last?
- What do I do now?

All these questions seem to come down to one thing: I'm scared!

There is nothing wrong with being scared. Though the questions you have may differ from those above, the common denominator is fear—fear of not making it, fear of loneliness, fear of tomorrow—and this fear comes at a time of life when you are at your most vulnerable. That's the bad news. The good news is that, even though you may not believe it right now, I have seen men and women in this situation, and who were ready to give up, go on and create for themselves a new life they cherish. A life they call their own.

How did these men and women get from a place of loss and fear to a new life?

By drawing on the faith and courage that reside in each of us. Remember, after a loss we must rejoin the world of the living. We don't have a choice! Bear in mind that your thoughts, words, and actions during this time have the power to make your life easier.

Despite my loss, I feel pretty clearheaded these days. Am I kidding myself?

To some degree, probably yes. I can't tell you how many times I have sat across from people who had just suffered losses and were starting over. I would review their situations and say, "OK, we have to do thus and such, and then we will do this and that, and finally this." They would agree with me, behaving as if they understood what I was saying, and I would take the necessary actions based on our conversation. Inevitably, six months to a year later, they would come back and say, "Can you tell me why we did what we did with the money?" It became obvious to me that they had not heard a word I had said during the early days of their grief. It was as if they had been present in body but not in mind. I would explain the reasons for the actions we took again, and this time they would finally get it.

What would you suggest doing financially after the basic issues have been taken care of?

Many of us emerge from a divorce or the death of a loved one with assets we must manage and protect, perhaps for the first time in our lives. After seeing the ways in which people tend to jeopardize these assets in their grief, their anger, their exhaustion, or their confusion, I have come up with a rule that has never once failed: Take no action with your money other than keeping it safe and sound for at least six months to a year after a loss.

Why do I need to wait six months to a year? I'm not that much of a basket case, am I?

One way or another, you have just been through a hard time, dealing with the legalities and expenses of divorce or the difficult tasks you've had to take on after a death. I am simply telling you that you are not equipped now—emotionally or financially—to make the big decisions that will have to be made. These include decisions about investing your money on your own or entrusting it to an adviser. If your money is in a secure place, a place that has allowed you to feel safe and comfortable about it until now, I want you to leave it there and to wait until your emotional equilibrium is restored before you take any action with your money. If you feel your money is *not* currently safe, make the financial changes that will get your money to a safe place, and then do nothing else for the time being.

How can I make sure that my money is being invested safely during this period?

My advice would be to seek out a financial adviser who comes highly recommended by a friend who has money under management with that adviser. If you have no friend who can recommend someone, what you want for now is a fee-based financial planner—one who does not sell products of any kind. When you go to see this adviser or planner, you may want to take a friend or relative with you for support. The first thing you should say is, "I am not going to buy anything for at least one year. I just want to make sure that the money I have is safe and sound. I want to put any money that is not safe now into a money-market fund or Treasuries, and that is all. No new purchases of any kind are to be made on my behalf."

What if I get a call from my late or ex-spouse's financial adviser?

I wouldn't be surprised if you did. Once a financial adviser has built a relationship with one partner, a separation or death gives him or her the opportunity to establish a rapport with the spouse who previously was merely a name on joint documents. Believe me, this opportunity is not lost on the adviser. Remember, this person has been aware of what went on not only with your money but also in your personal life. If there is to be a divorce, and therefore a dividing of the assets, the adviser is going to be one of the first to know what you each will be left with. If there is a death, the total picture of your finances is right at his or her disposal. So do not be surprised if you get a cozy call from an adviser with whom you have never really had a relationship to ask you to come in and see him or her to go over what to do with the money in your portfolio. But ask yourself this: How many times did the adviser or broker your spouse was using to manage your joint money talk to you before your world fell apart?

Should I talk to this financial adviser, or use the six-month plan that you suggested earlier?

You should wait. You're not ready. Just because your late spouse or ex-spouse was using a certain adviser does not mean that he or she will be the right adviser for you. I'm not suggesting that this adviser is necessarily wrong for you, only that this is your life, and everyone in it from this point on must be someone with whom you feel safe and comfortable. Ask yourself the following questions:

- Why was it that you never had a relationship with this particular person to begin with?
- If you did have a relationship with him/her, did you like and trust the relationship?
- Did you feel as if he/she had your best interests and concerns at heart, or just those of your spouse/partner?

Bide your time. These questions will answer themselves in due course.

So you're saying I should be careful with all people who will potentially have anything to do with my money?

Absolutely. Cold-callers, hungry brokers, and needy financial-planning types all read the obituaries to see if they can somehow expand their businesses. A sympathetic call when you are feeling vulnerable is often a self-interested call—and you're not the "self" in question here. Please say that you are grieving now and ask that solicitors who appear out of the blue call back in a year. They won't.

What about life insurance? Is there an optimal way to deal with my insurance company?

Yes. If you are entitled to any life insurance proceeds, regardless of the amount, take the payment in full, even if the insurance company tries to persuade you to take it in installments or offers to invest it or hold on to it for safekeeping. Most insurance proceeds are income tax–free, so you will not incur any penalties by taking them in a lump-sum payment. You may need to deposit some cash into a checking account right away to cover immediate expenses. Then put the rest into a money-market account or anywhere you know it will be safe but also accessible, in case you need funds for your living expenses. Leave the money there until you are more emotionally stable, so that you can intelligently decide what to do with it—again, six months to one year later.

What about making other big changes in my life? Should I put these off, too?

Yes, if you can. Over the next few months, I would like you to try to make as few changes in your life as possible. At the same time, I would also like you to begin asking yourself some essential questions. How do you feel about where you are living? Are you frightened by the amount of money it takes to live? Are there areas in which you could easily cut back your spending? In time, clarity will set in, and you will know what you must do, however painful, whether it's selling the house, taking a job or a second job, or cutting back on what you can do for your children. In time you will be able to do what you decide you need to do.

ADDITIONAL RESOURCES

BOOKS

The following books are indispensable, whether you are living together, separating, or getting a divorce.

Divorce & Money: How to Make the Best Financial Decisions During Divorce by attorneys Violet Woodhouse, CFP; Dale Fethering, and Victoria F. Collins, Ph.D., CFP; with M. C. Blakeman. Commonsense strategies for dividing debts, setting alimony, and much more.

Living Together: A Legal Guide for Unmarried Couples by attorneys Toni Lynne Ihara, Ralph E. Warner, and Frederick Hertz. Everything unmarried couples need to define and protect their relationship is covered in this superb resource.

Legal Affairs: Essential Advice for Same-Sex Couples by Frederick Hertz and Frank Browning.

A Legal Guide for Lesbian and Gay Couples by attorneys Hayden Curry, Denis Clifford, and Frederick Hertz. This excellent volume tells you all you need to make a living-together agreement, handle property, and much more.

INTERNET

Legal Information Institute, Cornell Law School
www.law.cornell.edu
Offers a huge database and search engine, as well as the complete text of various state court decisions.

Nolo
www.nolo.com/lawcenter/
The plain-English Law Center is a terrific resource for information on family legal matters.

Divorce Source
www.divorcesupport.com
This website contains an exhaustive resource of general and state-specific information.

FINDING PROFESSIONAL ADVICE

Lawyers

The best resource for evaluating lawyers in your region is the Martindale-Hubbell Directory, which is usually available at your local library. Or you can access the Martindale-Hubbell website at *www.martindale.com,* or their related site, *www.lawyers.com.*

You can reach the American Academy of Matrimonial Lawyers at 150 North Michigan Avenue, Suite 2040, Chicago, IL 60601. Their phone number is (312) 263-6477, and their fax number is (312) 263-7682. You can also access their website, *www .aaml.org.*

Mediation and Arbitration

One very good resource is The Center for Dispute Settlement, 1666 Connecticut Avenue NW, Suite 500, Washington, DC 20009. Their phone number is (202) 265-9572, and their fax number is (202) 332-3951. Or you can access their website, *www.cdsusa.org*.

The Association for Conflict Resolution is located at 1015 18th Street NW, Suite 1150, Washington, DC 20036. Their phone number is (202) 464-9700, and their website is *www.acrnet.org*.

Appraisers

American Society of Appraisers (business appraisers)
555 Herndon Parkway, Suite 125
Herndon, VA 20170
(703) 478-2228
www.appraisers.org

Appraisal Institute
550 W. Van Buren Street, Suite 1000
Chicago, IL 60607
(312) 335-4100
www.appraisalinstitute.com

The Kelley Blue Book (cars and used cars) can be accessed on the World Wide Web at *www.kbb.com*.

CHILD SUPPORT

The National Child Support Enforcement Association
444 North Capitol Street NW, Suite 414
Washington, DC 20001-1512

ADDITIONAL RESOURCES

(202) 624-8180
www.ncsea.org

Administration for Children and Families
U.S. Department of Health and Human Services
Child Support Enforcement
370 L'Enfant Promenade SW
Washington, DC 20447
(202) 401-9383
www.acf.dhhs.gov

TAX QUESTIONS AND ASSISTANCE

The Internal Revenue Service
(800) 829-1040
www.irs.gov

Taxes in Divorce
www.divorceinfo.com/taxes.htm

SOCIAL SECURITY

Social Security Administration
(800) 772-1213
www.ssa.gov

INDEX

ABOUT SUZE ORMAN

SUZE ORMAN has been called "a force in the world of personal finance" and a "one-woman financial advice powerhouse" by *USA Today*. A two-time Emmy® Award–winning television show host, *New York Times* best-selling author, magazine and online columnist, writer-producer, and motivational speaker, Suze is undeniably America's most recognized personal finance expert.

Suze has written five consecutive *New York Times* best sellers— *The Money Book for the Young, Fabulous & Broke*; *The Laws of Money, The Lessons of Life*; *The Road to Wealth*; *The Courage to Be Rich*; and *The 9 Steps to Financial Freedom*—as well as the national best sellers *Suze Orman's Financial Guidebook* and *You've Earned It, Don't Lose It*. Her most recent book, *Women & Money*, was published by Spiegel & Grau in February 2007. A newspaper column, also called "Women & Money," syndicated by Universal Press Syndicate, began in January 2007. Additionally, she has created *Suze Orman's FICO Kit, Suze Orman's Will & Trust*

Kit, *Suze Orman's Insurance Kit*, *The Ask Suze Library System*, and *Suze Orman's Ultimate Protection Portfolio*.

Suze has written, coproduced, and hosted five PBS specials based on her *New York Times* best-selling books. She is the single most successful fund-raiser in the history of public television, and recently won her second Daytime Emmy® Award in the category of Outstanding Service Show Host. Suze won her first Emmy® in 2004, in the same category.

Suze is a contributing editor to *O, The Oprah Magazine* and *O at Home* and has a biweekly column, "Money Matters," on Yahoo! Finance. Suze hosts her own award-winning national CNBC-TV show, *The Suze Orman Show*, which airs every Saturday night, as well as *Financial Freedom Hour* on QVC television.

Suze has been honored with three American Women in Radio and Television (AWRT) Gracie Allen Awards. This award recognizes the nation's best radio, television, and cable programming for, by, and about women. In 2003, Suze garnered her first Gracie for *The Suze Orman Show* in the National/Network/Syndication Talk Show category. She won her second and third Gracies in the Individual Achievement: Program Host category in 2005 and 2006.

Profiled in *Worth* magazine's 100th issue as among those "who have revolutionized the way America thinks about money," Suze also was named one of *Smart Money* magazine's top thirty "Power Brokers," defined as those who have most influenced the mutual fund industry and affected our money, in 1999. A 2003 inductee into the Books for a Better Life (BBL) Award Hall of Fame in recognition of her ongoing contributions to self-improvement, Suze previously received the 1999 BBL Motivational Book Award for *The Courage to Be Rich*. As a tribute to her continuing involvement, in 2002 the organization established the

Suze Orman First Book Award to honor a first-time author of a self-improvement book in any category. She received a 2003 Crossing Borders Award from the Feminist Press. The award recognizes a distinguished group of women who not only have excelled in remarkable careers but also have shown great courage, vision, and conviction by forging new places for women in their respective fields. In 2002, Suze was selected as one of five distinguished recipients of the prestigious TJFR Group News Luminaries Award, which honors lifetime achievement in business journalism.

A sought-after motivational speaker, Suze has lectured widely throughout the United States, South Africa, and Asia to audiences of up to fifty thousand people, often appearing alongside individuals such as Colin Powell, Rudy Giuliani, Jerry Lewis, Steve Forbes, and Donald Trump. She has been featured in almost every major publication in the United States and has appeared numerous times on *The View*, *Larry King Live*, and *The Oprah Winfrey Show*.

A Certified Financial Planner®, Suze directed the Suze Orman Financial Group from 1987 to 1997, served as vice president of investments for Prudential Bache Securities from 1983 to 1987, and from 1980 to 1983 was an account executive at Merrill Lynch. Prior to that, she worked as a waitress at the Buttercup Bakery in Berkeley, California, from 1973 to 1980.